Chakra Mindset

Personal Development through the Chakras

Antoniette Gomez

exhale
PUBLISHING

Exhale Publishing,
Canberra, ACT

Exhale Publishing

Canberra ACT

Orders: www.chakramindset.com

National Library of Australia Cataloguing-in-Publication entry

Author: Gomez, Antoniette, author.
Title: Chakra mindset : personal development through
               the chakras /

               Antoniette Gomez ; Laila Savolainen, artist.
ISBN: 9780992448004 (paperback)
Subjects: Chakras.

               Mind and body.

               Spiritual life.
Other Authors/Contributors: Savolainen, Laila Kristina, 1967- , illustrator.
Dewey Number: 131

This book is not intended as a substitute for the medical advice of physicians. The reader should regularly consult a physician in matters relating to his/her health and particularly with respect to any symptoms that may require diagnosis or medical attention.

Dear Kevin,

This book is dedicated to you

love your Positivity!

Antonette

xx

Contents

Acknowledgments

I would like to thank Laila Savolainen for your inspirational illustrations and dedication to the Chakra Mindset concept. I am truly grateful to have had you create such beautiful artwork based on many long conversations, unique interpretations and a remarkable intuitive connection.

To my wonderful teachers and mentors, thank you for feeding my desire to learn and for introducing me to new possibilities and the understanding that all is possible. A special mention to Suzie Williams, my Yoga teacher and mentor in all things Zen.

I would like to thank my Mum and Dad for being the most supportive and loving role models. You both share so much of yourselves selflessly, and I am forever grateful.

Peter, thank you for your reassurance and brotherly prodding. Sue, you are my twin flame, we are part of the same mould. You are me, and I am you.

My gorgeous Bianca, thank you for being you and understanding all that is me so effortlessly. Jamie, thank you for accompanying me each step of the way and for being my sounding board. Thank you both for your unconditional love and support. You are the greatest achievements of my life.

Last, but certainly not least, to my loving husband, my soul mate, thank you for being my companion and confidant for the past twenty seven years and always encouraging me to spread my wings and reach for the stars.

Foreword

The very first time I ever heard the word Chakra was back in 1974. I was nine years old and my teacher had the bright idea to offer yoga classes after school. I am not sure why this appealed to me, perhaps it was my family's connection with India, but I decided to sign up straight away.

There was this one moment in class when the teacher asked us to open up our 'Third Eye' Chakra and spread loving thoughts to children less fortunate than ourselves.

I remember being elated by this idea and feeling the light pouring out of my forehead and travelling across the seas to Africa and India. It felt like there was something I could do spiritually to comfort children rather than just eating everything on my plate; which had never made much sense to me.

Even though that may not seem particularly practical for those starving children at the time, that idea stayed with me and I now do charity work with children in Thailand with HIV. It just goes to show how powerful a strongly held intention can be and how that can influence the rest of our lives.

As the years went by I learnt more and more about Chakras and how they reflected areas of life. Root Chakra for survival and Sacral Chakra for sensual desire and so on. However, it was only when I met Antoniette Gomez that I started to see that knowledge of Chakras could be used as a fascinating and systematic approach to personal development and life coaching.

I first met Antoniette in 2011 when I taught her NLP and my own emotional clearing processes called Matrix Therapies®. She immediately stood out in class as being highly intelligent, warm and dynamic. Antoniette is one of those people who you bond with immediately and feel like you have known forever.

With her easy rapport and endless energy Antoniette was able to build her coaching and training business quickly and was highly sought after both personally and in the corporate and government arenas. She did this with seemingly effortless ease and grace.

I have always recognised in Antoniette a fellow pioneer, always questioning and seeking new ways of creating change.

Like the 60s and 70s, when yoga first became popular and there was a fusion of eastern and western philosophy, we live in an era of rapid change. People today are searching for a balance between success and spirituality. Most systems of change either focus on material goal setting without deeper meaning or on spiritual connection without measurable results.

What I love about Antoniette's approach, with Chakra Mindset, is her ability to bring spirituality and practicality together in a profound and meaningful way that still gets results in the material world.

With the breakdown of religion and family structures people are yearning for a connection with spirituality on their own terms. They don't want hierarchical institutions. They don't want to be told what to believe and how to live their lives; but at the same time they don't want to be rudderless without any way of navigating their own changes.

Chakra Mindset allows people to map their own changes in a way that suits each individual and yet is still systematic. It allows you to search for deeper meaning, happiness and peace in a way that gives you real outcomes in your day-to-day life.

I am so excited that you will be able to use these tools to begin to fulfil your potential and clearing blocks to your success and happiness.

I am also tremendously proud that Antoniette has decided to use my Matrix Therapies® as one of her therapeutic approaches. I look forward to hearing about the success stories that will come from reading and applying this material and wish you and Antoniette all the very best of fulfilment and happiness.

Pip McKay (BA Hons, Dip Ed Distinction)
CEO of Evolve Now! Mind Institute Pty Ltd and Archetype Academy®
Creator of Matrix Therapies® and Archetypal Coaching®
NLP Trainer and Coach
Co-founder of the Australian Board of NLP

Introduction

This book forms part of a personal development program that uses the chakra system as the structure to work through different areas of life. It has been developed as a companion to assist in systemising thoughts, priorities and individual aspirations.

The Chakra Mindset program includes:

- This Book – The Chakra Mindset book outlines the Chakra Mindset concept and includes information in regards to how to use the program in order to help you work towards reaching your goals and achieving the life of your dreams.

- The Journal – The Chakra Mindset journal has been developed as a companion to the book. The journal has space for reflection and to take notes in regards to your journey as you work through the program.

- Energy Intention Techniques audio – The energy intention techniques are guided activities that have been developed to assist individuals undertaking the Chakra Mindset program in releasing limiting beliefs, and setting intentions for the future.

- Meditations – The Chakra Mindset meditations include a

short guided meditation for each of the chakras and a longer meditation that reflects on all of the chakras.

All parts of the program are available for download via www.chakramindset.com.

The chakras provide a unique sequence of energy centres that have been combined with traditional personal development methodologies and Neuro-Linguistic Programming techniques, resulting in an effective and practical system that allows an individual to design a life of their dreams, set attainable goals and take the actions required to move their energy in the desired direction.

Chakras are an ancient system that have been studied and revered for thousands of years. The chakras are energy centres of spiritual power that are transfer points for our thoughts, feelings and specific functions of our organs. The word chakra is a Sanskrit word that means wheel, and signifies movement. There are seven major chakras that are connected with different areas of the body, stages of life and a wide range of physical and spiritual functions. The chakras govern different elements that manifest in the functionality and results that we see in our material world, as follows:

Root Chakra – Survival instincts, belonging, our environment and body

Sacral Chakra – Relationships, sensuality and the experience of pleasure

Solar Plexus Chakra – Manifestation, personal power and centre of joy

 Heart Chakra – Relationship with self and others, giving and receiving

 Throat Chakra – Communication and creativity

 Third Eye Chakra – Intuition and foresight

 Crown Chakra – Spirituality, connection, and purpose

Neuro-Linguistic Programing (NLP) is a personal development model that was developed in the 1970s by Richard Bandler and John Grinder. NLP is made up of techniques that assist individuals to make rapid and lasting change and empower them to take responsibility for their current and future results. I have used NLP techniques as the inspiration for some of the exercises throughout the book and program, including traditional NLP methods and additional modern techniques which involve Time Line Therapy® developed by Tad James and Matrix Therapies® developed by Pip McKay.

When I first started studying the chakras I saw them as individual wheels that were either in balance, overactive or deficient, and now I have an understanding that is far greater than any concept

I had ever imagined possible. This particular way of working with the chakras enables us to gain a deep understanding of our current situation; it is a method that assists us to reflect on the parts and the themes of each chakra that can help us to work toward clarity and balance. The Chakra Mindset program is unique in its approach, and the perspective taken when looking at the chakras stands apart due to the distinct method of viewing each of the chakras as one whole energy centre, and further breaking down each of the chakras into parts that represent different aspects of a whole energy centre.

The chakras are traditionally depicted as lotus blossoms. The Chakra Mindset has used the lotus blossoms as the foundation for breaking down each of the chakras, using the original number of lotus petals to represent the parts within each chakra that form the whole. Imagine a lotus flower with each petal representing a different aspect of the central bud, all working together towards a central balance, the parts that make a whole. Some of these parts are more developed because we spend our time, our energy and our focus in developing these parts, whilst other parts are less of a focus, and are therefore less intense. When these parts connect and join in the centre of our chakras, we have the whole result. For ease of practice when starting to use this program we have determined the number of parts for each of the chakras that when combined make a whole, but you may find as you start to practice this concept, you will have more or less parts that are of importance to you, that make up your ideal flow.

The Chakra Mindset is not meant to recreate the wheel or debunk any of the legends and traditions that make the chakras what they are; instead it is an alternate viewpoint, a different perspective for those who like to break things down in order to understand the multitude of possibilities at a deeper level. Breaking down the objective also eliminates the feeling of overwhelm often felt when dealing with change. Remember where focus goes energy flows.

The Chakra Mindset program has been designed to give you the space, tools and resources to evaluate your current position and life results, gain an understanding of the limitless possibilities that we have for change and growth, and incorporate practical concepts to work with. You may find that what can initially be experienced as an intense period of exploration and reflection, will then lead to co-designing the map that will enable you to create a future of your choice. The principles, exercises and techniques discussed can be, and are intended to be, used on a regular basis to maintain balance and harmony, and adapt to the changing tides in our lives; a companion for growth and reflection.

This book outlines some life strategies and exercises that when consistently practiced and implemented become as natural as breathing and eating. They will form part of your daily rituals, and assist you in finding success and fulfilment long term. Remember that life is a journey not a destination so be sure to stop and smell the flowers along the way.

The initial part of the program, Activating Your Chakra Mindset and Getting into Your Ideal Flow, will take approximately seven weeks to work through, one week for each chakra. The program has been designed so that you can work consecutively through each of your chakras from the Root Chakra making your way up to the Crown Chakra, or alternatively if you are experienced in working with your chakras you can start with any chakra you feel you would like to nurture, explore and balance.

Over time you may find that your priorities and your goals change, and again you can work through the processes listed to set an action plan. The program allows you to revisit areas of your life as things change and evolve. There is no end game, life is evolving and organic and so it is with you.

Each of us has a different ideal flow. This program is about finding yours.

Chapter 1

Getting to Know Your Chakras

The Root Chakra

The Root Chakra is located at the base of the spine; it is the energy centre that is our connection to the earth, stability and grounding. This chakra helps us feel connected to our roots. It is the centre of our survival, relationship with money, physical health and belonging; it represents our most primal survival instincts.

When the Root Chakra is balanced you have a sense of belonging, and you are safe in the knowledge that you are meant to be whom and where you are in your life.

The symbol for the Root Chakra is a lotus with four petals. The parts that make up the Root Chakra can either correspond to the number of petals, or it can be half of that which is two for ease of practice when starting to work with this concept.

The Sacral Chakra

The Sacral Chakra is located just below your navel. It is the centre of sensuality, relationships and desires. It rules our instinct and gut feelings as well as our emotions. It is the centre of balance that regulates our ability to give and receive. As with the Root Chakra, the Sacral Chakra is also connected to our survival instincts but extends past ourselves to include the survival needs of others in our family.

When the Sacral Chakra is balanced you express your feelings and emotions with ease, you experience a sense of pleasure and wellbeing, and are comfortable with your own sexuality and desires. You express your emotions easily.

The symbol for the Sacral Chakra is a lotus with six petals. The parts that make up the Sacral Chakra correspond to the number of petals, or it can be half of that which is three for ease of practice when starting to work with this concept.

The Solar Plexus Chakra

The Solar Plexus Chakra is located in the area above your navel. It is your centre of personal power and self-esteem. The Solar Plexus Chakra is the midway point between our spiritual and earthly aspects. It is associated with the ego and value of self and it is ruled by the conscious mind.

When the Solar Plexus Chakra is balanced you have a good level of confidence and are self-empowered. You are consciously creating your own reality and are good at manifesting what you desire. You have a good relationship with self and others and you trust your intuition and act upon your gut instincts.

The symbol for the Solar Plexus Chakra is a lotus with ten petals. The parts that make up the Solar Plexus Chakra correspond to the number of petals, or it can be half of that which is five for ease of practice when starting to work with this concept.

The Heart Chakra

The Heart Chakra is located in the centre of your chest. The Heart Chakra is the place that unconditional love and acceptance resides for both self and others. It is your centre of compassion, empathy and tolerance.

When the Heart Chakra is balanced you have compassion and consideration for all life. You are not ruled by your ego and can give and receive love unconditionally. You are fulfilled and living an abundant life.

The symbol for the Heart Chakra is a lotus with twelve petals. The parts that make up the Heart Chakra correspond to the number of petals, or it can be half of that which is six for ease of practice when starting to work with this concept.

The Throat Chakra

The Throat Chakra is located in the throat region. The Throat Chakra is your centre of communication and expression, allowing you to be creative and speak your truth; it is about listening as well as speaking.

When the Throat Chakra is balanced you are comfortable in expressing yourself through your words and communicating without fear of judgement or criticism.

The symbol for the Throat Chakra is a lotus with sixteen petals. The parts that make up the Throat Chakra correspond to the number of petals, or it can be half of that which is eight for ease of practice when starting to work with this concept.

The Third Eye Chakra

The Third Eye Chakra is located in the centre of the forehead between the eyes. The Third Eye Chakra is your centre of intuition, insight and wisdom. It is the place of imagination, enlightenment and knowing, allowing us to see past limitations and gain an understanding and connection to the universe.

When the Third Eye Chakra is balanced you trust your insight and intuition and expand your awareness and consciousness to encompass all that is.

The symbol for the Third Eye Chakra is a lotus with two large petals comprising of forty-eight smaller petals per large petal. The parts that make up the Third Eye Chakra is two, or if you are a beginner you can halve the number to one part for ease of practice when starting to work with this concept.

The Crown Chakra

The Crown Chakra is located at the top of the head. The Crown Chakra is our connection to the infinite source, the divine. It is our gateway to pure consciousness, and the meaning of this chakra is unique to each individual.

When the Crown Chakra is balanced we are living in harmony and unity with the entire universe, we are connected and living in peace being at one with the divine.

The symbol for the Crown Chakra is a thousand petal lotus. The parts that make up the Crown Chakra are infinite, therefore left to each individual to determine. If you are a beginner I recommend starting with one or two parts, and if you are experienced in working with the chakras you can have as many parts as you feel make up your ideal flow.

Activating the Chakra Mindset

Getting into Your Ideal Flow

Maintaining Your Ideal Flow

Reinventing Your Ideal Flow

Interaction and Process Flow

Read through the book and become familiar with the chakras and the four stages of the Chakra Mindset. It is recommended that you read through the individual chakra chapters (Chapter 3 through to 9) to get an understanding of each of the chakra traits and how they manifest in your life. These chapters also contain information regarding limiting beliefs, goal setting, energy intention techniques and rituals to increase your energy flow in each of the chakras. Revisit these areas and complete the interactive journal tasks once you have completed the Chakra State Analysis as outlined in Chapter 10 – Activating the Chakra Mindset.

Chapter 11 – Creating Your Ideal Flow explains the process you will need to follow to work with each of your chakras for a seven day period. Use your journal, mediations and interactive energy intention techniques to assist you whilst working through this stage of the Chakra Mindset.

Chapters 12 and 13 – Maintaining Your Ideal Flow and Creating Your Maintenance Plan outline the process you should follow incorporating the use of your journal to plan your maintenance phase.

Chapter 14 – Reinventing Your Ideal Flow explains the process for redesigning your goals and desired outcomes as you continue your journey of self-exploration and growth.

Chapter 2

The Four Stages of a Chakra Mindset

The Chakra Mindset program is divided into four stages. Each of the stages is uniquely designed in order to maximise your results as you work through the process.

Before moving onto the four stages of a Chakra Mindset you will need to take some time to read through each of the individual chakra chapters. These chapters will give you a good understanding of how the energy in each chakra centre flows when it is under stimulated, over stimulated or ideal for you. These chapters provide information on the chakras as well as exercises, techniques and rituals for you to become familiar with.

The structure and purpose of each of the stages are as follows:

Activating the Chakra Mindset

In this part of the program you will spend some time becoming familiar with your bridge point. Your bridge point is your starting point, where you are before you start the program. In order to determine your bridge point you will spend time working through the Chakra State Analysis on page 146. The Chakra State Analysis is a quiz that you can do in this book, the Chakra Mindset journal or online, to determine the current flow of energy in each of your chakras. You will then be encouraged to reflect on your results to date, determining what has worked well in the past and what areas of your life you would like to change. You will look at why you would like to make the changes and gain an understanding of the reasons behind the desired changes. For what purpose do you want things to be different? What is the outcome you seek going to give you?

Have you ever noticed that some people, perhaps even yourself, have the ideal flow or the perfect results in one area of their lives? It could be finances, it could be health, it may be relationships; this is usually an indication that a significant amount of time is being focused on one particular area, and that's great when it is well managed and does not become excessive. At times we focus all of our energy on one particular area of our lives leaving little energy or time for the other areas, thus resulting in a lack of balance and an uneven flow. Sometimes we can have it all in one particular area of our lives, yet still feel so unfulfilled, always feeling like there is something missing, looking for something more, whilst not being entirely sure what that may be. Once you are able to balance your energy flow and the results you are achieving across all areas of your life, you may notice that you start to feel a sense of balance, fulfilment and wholeness.

After completing the Activating the Chakra Mindset chapter you may have identified areas of your life that are working well. Alternatively you may have identified areas in which you would like to see some changes. The act of mindful observation and the focus of your attention and intention will assist in starting the flow of energy in the desired direction.

Getting into Your Ideal Flow

During this stage you will create an individualised plan for yourself as you are working with a particular chakra during the getting into your ideal flow period. It is recommended that you work through one chakra at a time for a period of seven days.

Even if a chakra centre is producing your ideal flow it is recommended that you work through the getting into your ideal flow process for all chakras.

You will identify limiting beliefs related to different areas of your life and challenge them. In order to create positive beliefs and thoughts that will help you move towards your ideal flow, you need to recognise and remove any current beliefs that are holding you back.

This stage includes journal time, energy intention techniques and guided meditations to help you explore, find and release that which no longer serves you. These processes are followed by creating your personalised action plan from the activities and rituals listed in each chakra chapter.

What we are aiming for is a balanced approach across all areas of your life; therefore we do not recommend focusing too much time in any one particular area. We encourage you to spend seven days focusing your energy on one chakra at a time. The Chakra Mindset is about creating flow and sustainable balance in all areas. If you focus too much attention in any one particular area you can create over activity. This too can create undesired results (see the over activity section in each of the individual chakra chapters).

Maintaining Your Ideal Flow

Once you have worked your way through the program and have completed the getting into your ideal flow stage for each of the chakras, the maintaining your ideal flow stage is the time when you start planning how you will maintain the flow. This is done through incorporating the practices into your daily life in a manageable and practical manner. This part of the program is about lifestyle. Every successful person has rituals and practices that allow them to continue getting the results that they have worked towards.

When working through this stage it is a good time to reflect back on your bridge point and prioritise each of the areas of your life. It may be unrealistic to expect that you want to be performing in all areas of your life at 100%. However, by this point you will have a healthy understanding of the need to pay attention to all areas. This does not mean that you will not have priorities.

Once you have prioritised each area you will then create a maintenance plan that is reflective of the priorities you have set. For example, if your top priority was the Heart Chakra you would want to ensure that you include a Heart Chakra activity into your daily practices; some of the other activities for the other chakras may fall into weekly or even monthly practices.

This stage of the program will explain how you can continue to have a consistent flow without creating any areas of blockages or over stimulation. Every area needs attention and it's up to you to decide how much is right for you and your ideal lifestyle.

Reinventing Your Ideal Flow

Once you have worked with this program for some time, you may begin to feel adventurous and want to achieve even greater and bigger things than you had initially identified. This is precisely the aim of this program; to allow you to have additional resources and processes to help you on your journey of self-discovery and growth.

In this section of the program you are shown how to go back and re-evaluate your bridge point and change or add to the existing parts originally selected to determine your ideal flow. Remember, it is okay to change your desires and priorities as your life changes. It's about identifying what's good for you and having the courage to take the steps required to initiate these changes.

Chapter 3

Getting to Know Your Chakras – Root Chakra

Root Chakra Summary Chart

Names	Root Chakra, Muladhara
Symbol	Lotus flower with four petals
Location	Base of spine
Element	Earth
Sense	Smell
Plane	Physical plane
Colour	Red
Ruling Planet	Mars

The Root or First Chakra is commonly referred to as the survival chakra; it is the energy centre of belonging, connection and our physical health. The element of the Root Chakra is the earth and the objective of this chakra is quite primal in nature. It's about self-preservation and ensuring we have enough food, money and shelter to survive. This chakra is the centre of our belonging, either to our family group, society or humanity as a whole.

The Root Chakra is the energy centre that dictates our relationship with the environment, giving us a sense of grounding and attachment. Our relationship with mother earth begins here and when nurtured we feel comfortable and confident.

Balanced Root Chakra

When you have a balanced Root Chakra you have a healthy sense of belonging, are comfortable with your body shape and size and have a healthy relationship with money and food. You feel safe in your environment, are comfortable manifesting and working towards your desires. You have energy and a motivation to work towards your objectives and a strong connection with family and friends.

Underactive Root Chakra

When your Root Chakra is underactive you may have feelings of insecurity, often feel overwhelmed and may suffer from anxiety. You have a poor relationship with food and are self-conscious. You struggle with finances, have a tendency to overthink everything and a tendency to worry unnecessarily. You feel like an outsider and that you do not belong. You may feel underserving and not good enough.

Overactive Root Chakra

An overactive Root Chakra can manifest in a number of ways these may include, hoarding type behaviour and an aggressive and cynical nature. An overactive Root Chakra can lead to dominant behaviour, often feeling the need to belittle others to prove that you are superior. You may be opinionated and be very inflexible to change. You may have weight and body issues.

NB: Some symptoms of an overactive and underactive chakra can be similar, or interchangeable. Simply read each of the patterns to see what you relate to. When we are working on increasing the energy flow in any area, remember it is OK to increase positive energy, even if you feel you may have the symptoms of an overactive chakra. The positive energy will reverse the impact of the overactive negative energy because it is coming from a place of thriving rather than a place of just surviving.

Physical Issues of an Unbalanced Root Chakra

The Root Chakra governs our feet, legs, hips, spine and immune system.

Some of the physical indicators of an unbalanced Root Chakra may include:

- Addictive behaviours
- Lower back problems
- Rectal issues
- Diarrhoea
- Impotence
- Conditions involving the hips, groin, legs and feet
- Poor circulation
- Bone problems
- Depression
- Eczema
- Weight issues
- Lower intestine problems

The Parts that Make the Whole

The symbol for the Root Chakra is a lotus with four petals. The parts that make up the Root Chakra can either correspond to the number of petals or can be half of that, which is two, if you are starting out on your journey. Or it may be as many parts as you feel are required for your ideal flow in the Root Chakra. Expanding on the number of parts is recommended once you have become familiar with the Chakra Mindset concept.

Limiting Beliefs

Limiting beliefs and the limiting beliefs release technique is explained in detail in Chapter 11 Getting into Your Ideal Flow.

The list below provides some examples of limiting beliefs that could cause your Root Chakra to not function at its best:

- I do not belong
- I am not smart enough
- I am not good looking enough
- I am stupid
- I am afraid of doing new things because it will only lead to disappointment
- I am not worthy
- Nobody loves me
- The world is unsafe
- Having everything I want is impossible
- I am unlovable

- I am not good enough
- It's not OK to be rich
- I can't make money doing something I love
- It's survival of the fittest, therefore I have to be aggressive
- If I let my guard down people will take advantage of me
- It's a sign of weakness to be compassionate
- Conforming means I lose control

Goal Setting - SMART Goal Example

Goal setting and SMART goals are explained in detail in Chapter 11 Getting into Your Ideal Flow.

As part of the goal setting process the following is an example of a SMART goal.

Part – Good Relationship with Money

Mini Goal – Create a monthly budget for use to manage household funds. The budget will take into consideration all expenses and income and it will give me the opportunity to accurately record transactions. I will complete the budget by Friday of this week.

 Journal

Focused Intention Technique

The focused intention technique is explained in detail in Chapter 11 Getting into Your Ideal Flow.

Decide on up to three states you would like to stack as part of your process for creating your Root Chakra Point. Use your parts as inspiration for these states.

An example of how to use parts chosen to develop your Root Chakra Point is as follows:

Three of the parts that you may have chosen to work on in the Root Chakra:

- Trust
- Healthy
- Excited

If you have two parts, create two states to stack and if you have four parts or more choose up to three parts. An example of states to use to reinforce these parts may be to recall a time when:

- You felt like you really trusted yourself, and the outcome was positive
- You felt really healthy
- You felt really excited

We are looking for distinct, separate occasions for each state you would like to stack. If you cannot recall a time when you felt what you would like to achieve, I would like you to imagine what it would feel like. Do try to recall a natural state in the first instance as this is far more effective. Write your three states in your *Journal*

Activities to Balance Your Root Chakra

Morning Moments – The practice of morning moments gives you a great start to the day and takes minimal time to complete. The entire process takes under five minutes. Morning moments are a combination of your gratitude practice, your mantras and visualisations.

Gratitude Practice – A gratitude practice is the practice of taking some time each day to list what you are grateful for. In relation to your Root Chakra, some of the things you may choose to be grateful for may include:

- Your connection to others (family, friends, pets, colleagues, etc.)
- Your environment
- Your health
- Your job
- Being alive
- The food on the table

This simple practice of gratitude gives you the space to stop and appreciate what you have. Gratitude will attract more things in your life to be grateful for. A good practice to get into either first thing in the morning or last thing before you go to bed is to simply acknowledge and be grateful for the things you have.

Another great way of doing this is to keep a picture of all the things you are grateful for. You may want to start by taking one photo a day; spend some time reflecting and looking over these pictures. The more you look for things to be grateful for the more you will find.

Mantras – Creating mantras that you can repeat daily either as part of your morning moments or meditation process is a powerful and effective method of bringing your desired intentions into reality.

A good way to create mantras is to use your chosen chakra parts and insert an 'I am', or an 'I' in front of the phrase. For example:

- Belonging – I belong
- Abundant – I am abundant
- Grounded – I am grounded
- Family connection – I am connected to family

Visualising your ideal day – Take the time to visualise, feel and create your ideal day. Imagine feeling and seeing your interactions with others, your results and how you would like the events of the day to play out.

Essential Oils

Essential oils have been used for thousands of years to treat both mental and physical conditions; there are various essential oils that are recommended for each of the chakras. The predominant sense for the Root Chakra is the sense of smell, therefore I would highly recommend including the use of essential oils when working with this chakra.

Some of the uses for essential oils may include:

- Aromatherapy – diffusing oils
- Essential oil baths
- Essential oil massages
- Essential oil creams
- Essential oil mists

Some therapeutic grade essential oils can be applied directly to the skin and some high-grade therapeutic essential oils can even be ingested; however, you would need to confirm with the manufacturer the grade and quality of the oils as well as confirm the recommended uses.

You could experiment by combining two or three of the recommended essential oils into a carrier cream and use the cream as hand moisturiser whilst you are working with the Root Chakra.

Essential oils that are particularly good when working with the Root Chakra include:

- Cedarwood
- Sandalwood
- Vetiver
- Clove
- Myrrh
- Patchouli
- Pine
- Rosemary

You may find other oils that stimulate your Root Chakra. Go towards scents that you feel are earthy and have a connection to mother earth.

Crystals

The use of crystals as healing and divination tools goes back centuries. Crystals can be used for meditation, healing, reflection, simply as an ornament to beautify a space or a piece of jewellery. Crystals can absorb and transmute negative energy and are great to use when you are focusing on your chakras.

Some of the uses for Crystals when working with the chakras may include:

- Meditation
- Carrying the crystal in a bag or pocket
- Wearing the crystal in a piece of jewellery
- Keeping the crystals in your environment
- Crystal therapy – You may wish to see a practitioner for a crystal chakra balance. You will find most alternate therapists can assist with this service

Different crystals have different healing attributes. Some of the crystals recommended when working with your Root Chakra include:

- Garnet
- Ruby
- Obsidian
- Hematite

❀ Red Jasper
❀ Smokey Quartz
❀ Black Tourmaline

You may be drawn to other crystals when you are working with your Root Chakra, trust your instincts. You may find other crystals that are predominately red in colour that you may choose to work with.

Physical Exercises

Your Root Chakra is the centre for physical health. Any type of exercise would be a great inclusion to your daily program when working with the Root Chakra. Like any physical program you should consult your doctor before starting a new regime.

Some exercises recommended specifically for the Root Chakra include:

❀ Jogging
❀ Fast walking
❀ Walking in nature
❀ Strengthening exercises
❀ Team sports

Yoga Poses

Yoga poses recommended for working on your Root Chakra, include the Mountain Pose and the Warrior Pose.

Mountain Pose

1. Stand barefoot on your mat or outside (outside on the grass would be ideal), your upper body should be relaxed yet upright and straight;

2. Bring your awareness to your breath, inhale deeply and slowly all the way into your lower belly, continue taking deliberate deep slow breaths;

3. Feel the earth under your feet, place your feet shoulder width apart and parallel, wriggle your toes and spread them apart, keeping knees soft;

4. Imagine roots flowing from your feet deep down into the earth, feel the connection and the stability of the roots;

5. Continue breathing slowly and deeply focusing on your connection to the earth and at the same time visualise a beautiful red disc at the base of your spine glowing, pulsating and expanding.

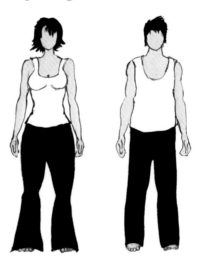

Warrior Pose

1. Start with a lunge position, foot facing forward with the front knee bent and above the ankle and the back leg straight with foot on 45 degree angle, your head should be facing in the same direction as your bent knee and your torso should be facing forwards;

2. Raise your arms straight out to the sides to shoulder height;

3. Feel the connection to the earth through your feet and the strength rising up through your torso, hold for 20 to 40 seconds in each direction whilst you continue breathing slowly and deeply focusing on your connection to the earth whilst at the same time visualising a beautiful red disc at the base of your spine glowing, pulsating and expanding.

Other Activities to Activate and Maintain Your Flow in the Root Chakra

Clothing – Wearing red clothing and accessories can help stimulate your Root Chakra. Have fun with this! I will often have a coloured day, depending on the chakra I am working with at the time.

Gardening – Spending time in the garden and getting your hands in the dirt, planting and nurturing plants and/or vegetables is an effective way to restore your connection to mother earth.

Creating a budget – Working on a budget is a good way to start becoming familiar with the concept that you can control the financial situation, and that it doesn't have to be the other way around. Doing some simple budgeting practices gives you control and a clearer picture of your financial situation.

Mindful Eating – You may think that perhaps you enjoy your food too much, but if you choose to be aware and in the moment when you are eating, the experience can have a completely different effect.

Incorporating these simple rules can help improve your relationship with food:

- ❀ Eat only when you are hungry
- ❀ Enjoy what you are eating and chew your food
- ❀ Be mindful of your portions

- Include fruit and vegetables in your diet
- You do not have to finish all the food on your plate
- Try eating the best bits first rather than last

Meditations – Meditations are useful for connecting with your higher self and allowing yourself space and time to reflect. If you have never meditated you do not have to be a Zen Monk to practice the art of meditation; you can simply follow along with a guided meditation and take the time out to focus your intentions. There are many guided meditations available for use.

The Chakra Mindset meditations CD and mp3 downloads have a short meditation of up to fifteen minutes for each chakra. Take the time each day to complete the meditation relevant to the chakra you are working with.

Chapter 4

Getting to Know Your Chakras – Sacral Chakra

Sacral Chakra Summary Chart

Names	Sacral Chakra, Svadhishthana
Symbol	Lotus flower with six petals
Location	Two inches under the navel
Element	Water
Sense	Taste
Plane	Astral plane
Colour	Orange
Ruling Planet	Mercury

The Sacral or Second Chakra is commonly referred to as the chakra of sensuality; it is the energy centre of our sexuality, our feelings and our emotions. Like the Root Chakra it is also a lower chakra that is concerned with our survival needs. However, it extends past our own needs to include our families. It is located just two inches under the navel in your lower abdomen. The element of the Sacral Chakra is water and it is often referred to as the essence of life.

This chakra is the centre of our relationship with pleasure and desire. It is about receiving and giving yourself freely and being comfortable with intimacy.

Balanced Sacral Chakra

When you have a balanced Sacral Chakra you enjoy life, you have a good self-image and are comfortable with your sexuality and expressing your feelings. You express yourself through your creativity and your emotions without the need to overstate things; you take people's feelings into consideration without putting their needs before your own. You are playful, expressive and are comfortable with intimacy.

Underactive Sacral Chakra

When your Sacral Chakra is underactive you may be quiet, shy and withdrawn; you feel guilt or shame in expressing your sexuality. You have low self-esteem, are uncomfortable with intimacy and expressing your emotions and feelings. You may lack creativity and feel generally sluggish. You tend to deny yourself any activity or thing that may bring you pleasure.

Overactive Sacral Chakra

An overactive Sacral Chakra can manifest in a number of ways.

These may include: being over emotional, having a tendency to create drama in your life and to manipulate and crave power. You may have sexual, alcohol, tobacco or other addictions; with a tendency to overindulge in many areas of your life.

NB: Some symptoms of an overactive and underactive chakra can be similar, or interchangeable, simply read each of the patterns to see what you relate to. When we are working on increasing the energy flow in any area, remember it is OK to increase positive energy, even if you feel you may have the symptoms of an overactive chakra. The positive energy will reverse the impact of the overactive negative energy, because it is coming from a place of thriving rather than a place of just surviving.

Physical Issues of an Unbalanced Sacral Chakra

The Sacral Chakra governs our sexual organs, reproductive organs, spleen, kidney, gallbladder, respiratory system, and lower back.

Some of the physical indicators of an unbalanced Sacral Chakra may include:

- Menstrual problems
- Irritable bowel syndrome
- Problems with sexual organs
- Bladder problems
- Candida

- Kidney issues
- Frigidity
- Prostate problems

The Parts that Make the Whole

The symbol for the Sacral Chakra is a lotus with six petals. The parts that make up the Sacral Chakra can either correspond to the number of petals, or can be half of that, which is three, if you are starting out on your journey. Or it may be as many parts as you feel are required for your ideal flow in the Sacral Chakra. Expanding on the number of parts is recommended once you have become familiar with the Chakra Mindset concept.

Limiting Beliefs

The list below provides some examples of limiting beliefs that could cause your Sacral Chakra to not function at its best:

- I am not wanted
- I am frigid
- I am not worthy
- I am undesirable
- I am afraid of relationships because they don't work
- Sex is bad
- Sex is dirty

- I do not deserve good things
- If I allow myself to feel, I will lose control
- I am unlovable
- I am not good enough
- It's not OK to enjoy intimacy
- You can't trust anyone but yourself
- Life wasn't meant to be easy
- If I show people my true self they won't like me
- If I don't have it now I may not have the opportunity again
- Feeling pleasure is selfish

Goal Setting – SMART Goal Example

As part of the goal setting process the following is an example of a SMART goal.

Part – Self-Nurturing

Mini Goal – I will book in for a massage or a mini facial on a monthly basis. I will do this on the third Friday of every month.

Journal

Focused Intention Technique

Decide on up to three states you would like to stack as part of your process for creating your Sacral Chakra Point. Use your parts as inspiration for these states.

An example of how to use parts chosen to develop your Sacral Chakra Point is as follows:

Three of the parts that you may have chosen to work on in the Sacral Chakra:

- Playful
- Enjoy Sex
- Free

An example of states to use to reinforce these parts may be to recall a time when:

- You felt really playful and had a great time
- You really allowed yourself to enjoy sex
- You felt really free

We are looking for distinct, separate occasions for each state you would like to stack. If you cannot recall a time when you felt what you would like to achieve, I would like you to imagine what it would feel like. Do try to recall a natural state in the first instance as this is far more effective. Write your three states in your *Journal*

Activities to Balance Your Sacral Chakra

Morning Moments – The practice of morning moments gives you a great start to the day and takes minimal time to complete. The entire process takes under five minutes. Morning moments are a combination of your gratitude practice, your mantras and visualisations.

Mantras – Creating mantras that you can repeat daily either as part of your morning moments or meditation process is a powerful and effective method of bringing your desired intentions into reality.

A good way to create mantras is to use your chosen chakra parts, and insert an 'I am', or an 'I' in front of the phrase. For example:

- Pleasure – I enjoy feeling pleasure
- Good relationships with others – I have good relationships with others
- Sensual – I feel sensual
- Worthy – I am worthy

Gratitude Practice – A gratitude practice is the practice of taking some time each day to list what you are grateful for. In relation to your Sacral Chakra, some of the things you may choose to be grateful for may include:

- Your connection to others (lovers, partners, family, friends, pets, colleagues, etc.)
- Your body

- Your vitality
- Yourself
- Being alive
- Your energy
- The good things in life
- Your ability to express yourself
- Your relationships

This simple practice of gratitude gives you the space to stop and appreciate what you have. Gratitude will attract more things in your life to be grateful for. A good practice to get into either first thing in the morning or last thing before you go to bed is to simply acknowledge and be grateful for the things you have.

Another great way of doing this is to keep a picture of all the things you are grateful for. You may want to start by taking one photo a day; spend some time reflecting and looking over these pictures. The more you look for things to be grateful for the more you will find.

Visualising your ideal day – Take the time to visualise, feel and create your ideal day. Imagine feeling and seeing your interactions with others, your results, and how you would like the events of the day to play out.

Essential Oils

Essential oils have been used for thousands of years to treat both mental and physical conditions; there are various essential oils that are recommended for each of the chakras.

Some of the uses for essential oils may include:

- Aromatherapy – diffusing oils
- Essential oil baths
- Essential oil massages
- Essential oil creams
- Essential oil mists

Some therapeutic grade essential oils can be applied directly to the skin and some high grade therapeutic essential oils can even be ingested; however, you would need to confirm with the manufacturer the grade and quality of the oils, as well as confirm the recommended uses.

You could experiment by combining two or three of the recommended essential oils into a carrier cream and use the cream as hand moisturiser whilst you are working with the Sacral Chakra.

Essential oils that are particularly good when working with the Sacral Chakra include:

- Jasmine
- Geranium

- Orange
- Melissa
- Sandalwood

You may find other oils that stimulate your Sacral Chakra. Go towards scents that you feel are sensual and enjoyable.

Crystals

The use of crystals as healing and divination tools goes back centuries. Crystals can be used for meditation, healing, reflection, or simply as an ornament to beautify a space or a piece of jewellery. Crystals can absorb and transmute negative energy and are great to use when you are focusing on your chakras.

Some of the uses for crystals when working with the chakras may include:

- Meditation
- Carrying the crystal in a bag or pocket
- Wearing the crystal in a piece of jewellery
- Keeping the crystals in your environment
- Crystal therapy – You may wish to see a practitioner for a crystal chakra balance. You will find most alternate therapists can assist with this service

Different crystals have different healing attributes. Some of the crystals recommended when working with your Sacral Chakra include:

- Orange Calcite
- Tiger's Eye
- Moonstone
- Orange Jasper
- Amber
- Mookaite
- Carnelian

You may be drawn to other crystals when you are working with your Sacral Chakra, trust your instincts. You may find other crystals that are predominately orange in colour that you may choose to work with.

Physical Exercises

Your Sacral Chakra is the centre of pleasure, allowing yourself to feel good. Any type of exercise would be a great inclusion to your daily program when working with the Sacral Chakra. Like any physical program you should consult your doctor before starting a new regime.

Some exercises recommended specifically for the Sacral Chakra include:

- Yoga
- Swimming
- Walking or hiking in nature or on the beach

Stretching and toning exercises
 Dancing

Yoga Poses

Yoga Poses recommended for working on your Sacral Chakra, include the Goddess Pose and the Cobra Pose.

Goddess Pose

1. Stand in the mountain pose, and now open your legs about three feet apart, turn your heels in, toes pointing out;
2. Bend your knees coming into a wide squat; your thighs should be parallel to the ground and your knees directly above your ankles;
3. Raise your arms up to shoulder height and bend your elbows to ninety degrees;
4. Continue breathing slowly for a count of five whilst deeply focusing on your Sacral Chakra and at the same time visualise a beautiful orange disc just under your navel, glowing, pulsating and expanding.

Cobra Pose

1. Lying face down on the ground with legs extended behind you;

2. Place hands under your shoulders with fingers pointing to the top of your mat, hug elbows in to the sides of your body;

3. Press down through your pubic bone and the tops of your feet;

4. Inhale and lift your head and chest off the floor;

5. Draw shoulders back and gently straighten your arms (only straighten to a comfortable position), keep shoulders dropped away from your ears. Hold the pose for 30 seconds.

NB: This pose should be avoided if you have back or disc problems.

Other Activities to Activate and Maintain Your Flow in the Sacral Chakra

Clothing – Wearing orange clothing and accessories can help stimulate your Sacral Chakra. Have fun with this! I will often have a coloured day, depending on the chakra I am working with at the time.

Dancing – Any type of free flowing movement that allows you to express yourself. Dance like no one is watching and enjoy the freedom of movement.

Playing – Be playful. Do any activity just for the fun of it; this could include: riding, skipping, singing etc., or anything that brings you joy.

Explore different tastes – The predominant sense of the Sacral Chakra is taste. Take some time to explore different tastes; you may want to try different cultural foods and drinks.

Get creative – Try your hand at some creative activities. You may wish to draw, take up some crafts, or explore any activity that allows you to be creative.

Water – As the main element for the Sacral Chakra is water you may wish to increase the amount of water you are drinking and spend more time near water. If you do not live near water take a bath or have longer showers, allowing yourself to enjoy the sensation of the water.

Meditations – Meditations are useful for connecting with your higher self and allowing yourself space and time to reflect. If you have never meditated you do not have to be a Zen Monk to practice the art of meditation; you can simply follow along with a guided meditation and take the time out to focus your intentions. There are many guided meditations available for use.

The Chakra Mindset meditations have a short meditation of up to fifteen minutes for each chakra. Take the time each day to complete the meditation relevant to the chakra you are working with.

Chapter 5

Getting to Know Your Chakras – Solar Plexus Chakra

Solar Plexus Chakra Summary Chart

Names	Solar Plexus, Manipura
Symbol	Lotus flower with ten petals
Location	Above the navel and below the sternum
Element	Fire
Sense	Sight
Plane	Celestial plane
Colour	Yellow
Ruling Planet	Sun

The Solar Plexus or Third Chakra is often referred to as the chakra of your personal power, control and who you are; this is where your self-esteem and ego reside. It is located above your navel just below your sternum. It is also your energy centre of intuition, your place of knowing and doing what feels right.

This chakra is the centre of enthusiasm and drive. It houses your ability to manifest and control the direction of your life. It sits in the centre of our bodies between our upper and lower chakras, where our physical aspects meet our higher selves. It is ruled by the conscious mind.

Balanced Solar Plexus Chakra

When you have a balanced Solar Plexus Chakra you have energy and a sense of purpose, you act in a proactive rather than reactive manner, creating opportunities and following through. You have the ability to choose the direction of things in your life and make the most of opportunities.

You trust your gut instincts and have high self-esteem; you assert your power in a respectful manner, showing respect for both yourself and others. You are courageous, disciplined and are able to turn your ambitions into reality.

Underactive Solar Plexus Chakra

When your Solar Plexus Chakra is underactive you may lack self-confidence, you fear rejection and allow yourself to be controlled by others. You do not trust your intuition and act out of a sense of obligation. You may be overly concerned about the opinion of others and are affected by the negative moods of those around you.

You may have a sense of floating through life with no real sense of direction or orientation and no will power to follow through, even if you have something to work towards.

Overactive Solar Plexus Chakra

When your Solar Plexus Chakra energy is excessive you can be quite egotistical, feeling the need to control and dominate others. You show disregard for those around you and are overly concerned with demonstrating your power and position. You react with emotional outbursts and are often stressed and agitated.

NB: Some symptoms of an overactive and underactive chakra can be similar, or interchangeable. Simply read each of the patterns to see what you relate to. When we are working on increasing the energy flow in any area, remember it is OK to increase positive energy, even if you feel you may have the symptoms of an overactive chakra. The positive energy will reverse the impact of the overactive negative energy, because it is coming from a place of thriving rather than a place of just surviving.

Physical Issues of an Unbalanced Solar Plexus Chakra

The Solar Plexus Chakra governs the digestive system, adrenals, liver and skin.

Some of the physical indicators of an unbalanced Solar Plexus Chakra may include:

- Digestive problems
- Food allergies
- Arthritis
- Gallstones

- Liver disease
- Anaemia
- Pancreatitis
- Diabetes

The Parts that Make the Whole

The symbol for the Solar Plexus Chakra is a lotus with ten petals. The parts that make up the Solar Plexus Chakra can either correspond to the number of petals, or can be half of that, which is five, if you are starting out on your journey. Or, it may be as many parts as you feel are required for your ideal flow in the Solar Plexus Chakra. Expanding on the number of parts is recommended once you become familiar with the Chakra Mindset concept.

Limiting Beliefs

The list below provides some examples of limiting beliefs that could cause your Solar Plexus Chakra to not function at its best:

- I am not good
- I am weak
- I am not worthy
- I am undesirable
- I am afraid to succeed
- I don't have what it takes

- Power is bad
- I have no ambition
- Why try, I will only fail
- I am not good enough
- If it's helping others I can't make money doing it
- Other people are better than me
- Life wasn't meant to be easy
- I am scared of success
- I am scared of failure

Goal Setting – SMART Goal Example

As part of the goal setting process the following is an example of a SMART goal.

Part – High Self-Esteem

Mini Goal – I will develop a mantra about self-love and repeat it to myself three times daily in front of the mirror for the seven days I am working with my Solar Plexus Chakra.

Journal

Focused Intention Technique

Decide on up to three states you would like to stack as part of your process for creating your Solar Plexus Chakra Point. Use your parts as inspiration for these states.

An example of how to use parts chosen to develop your Solar Plexus Chakra Point is as follows:

71

Three of the parts that you may have chosen to work on in the Solar Plexus Chakra:

- Willpower
- Trust Intuition
- Strong

An example of states to use to reinforce these parts may be to recall a time when:

- You used your willpower to achieve something you were working towards
- You really trusted your intuition and it served you well
- You felt strong

We are looking for distinct, separate occasions for each state you would like to stack. If you cannot recall a time when you felt what you would like to achieve, I would like you to imagine what it would feel like. Do try to recall a natural state in the first instance as this is far more effective. Write your three states in your *Journal*

Activities to Balance Your Solar Plexus Chakra

Morning Moments – The practice of morning moments gives you a great start to the day and takes minimal time to complete. The entire process takes under five minutes. Morning moments are a combination of your gratitude practice, your mantras and visualisations.

Gratitude Practice – A gratitude practice is the practice of taking some time each day to list what you are grateful for. In relation to your Solar Plexus Chakra, some of the things you may choose to be grateful for may include:

- Your achievements
- Your career
- Your purpose in life
- Yourself
- Being alive
- Your energy
- The good things in life
- Your ability to manifest your reality
- Your perseverance

This simple practice of gratitude gives you the space to stop and appreciate what you have. Gratitude will attract more things in your life to be grateful for. A good practice to get into either first thing in the morning or last thing before you go to bed is to simply acknowledge and be grateful for the things you have.

Another great way of doing this is to keep a picture of all the things you are grateful for. You may want to start by taking one photo a day; spend some time reflecting and looking over these pictures. The more you look for things to be grateful for the more you will find.

Mantras – Creating mantras that you can repeat daily either as part of your morning moments or meditation process is a powerful and effective method of bringing your desired intentions into reality.

A good way to create mantras is to use your chosen chakra parts, and insert an 'I am', or an 'I' in front of the phrase. For example:

- High self-esteem – I have high self-esteem
- Willpower – I have strong willpower
- Confident – I am confident
- Fulfilled – I am fulfilled

Visualising your ideal day – Take the time to visualise, feel and create your ideal day. Imagine feeling and seeing your interactions with others, your results, and how you would like the events of the day to play out.

Essential Oils

Essential oils have been used for thousands of years to treat both mental and physical conditions; there are various essential oils that are recommended for each of the chakras.

Some of the uses for essential oils may include:

- Aromatherapy – diffusing oils
- Essential oil baths
- Essential oil massages
- Essential oil creams
- Essential oil mists

Some therapeutic grade essential oils can be applied directly to the skin and some high grade therapeutic essential oils can even be ingested; however, you would need to confirm with the manufacturer the grade and quality of the oils, as well as confirm the recommended uses.

You could experiment by combining two or three of the recommended essential oils into a carrier cream and use the cream as hand moisturiser whilst you are working with the Solar Plexus Chakra.

Essential oils that are particularly good when working with the Solar Plexus Chakra include:

- Basil
- Ginger
- Bergamot
- Chamomile

You may find other oils that stimulate your Solar Plexus Chakra. Go towards scents that you feel are inspiring and uplifting.

Crystals

The use of crystals as healing and divination tools goes back centuries. Crystals can be used for meditation, healing, reflection or simply as an ornament to beautify a space or a piece of jewellery. Crystals can absorb and transmute negative energy and are great to use when you are focusing on your chakras.

Some of the uses for crystals when working with the chakras may include:

- Meditation
- Carrying the crystal in a bag or pocket
- Wearing the crystal in a piece of jewellery
- Keeping the crystals in your environment
- Crystal therapy – You may wish to see a practitioner for a crystal chakra balance. You will find most alternate therapists can assist with this service

Different crystals have different healing attributes. Some of the crystals recommended when working with your Solar Plexus Chakra include:

- Tiger's Eye
- Citrine
- Yellow Topaz
- Yellow Sapphire
- Sulphur
- Serpentine
- Yellow Jasper

You may be drawn to other crystals when you are working with your Solar Plexus Chakra, trust your instincts. You may find other crystals that are predominately yellow in colour that you may choose to work with.

Physical Exercises

The following is a list of exercises you may wish to choose from when working on your Solar Plexus Chakra. Like any physical program you should consult your doctor before starting a new regime.

Some exercises recommended specifically for the Solar Plexus Chakra include:

- Yoga
- Strengthening exercises

- Rock climbing
- Spending time outdoors
- Martial Arts
- Pilates

Yoga Poses

Yoga Poses recommended for working on your Solar Plexus Chakra, include the Cow Pose and the Cat Pose.

Cow Pose

1. Start on your hands and knees with your back flat in a table top position, making sure your knees are directly below your hips. Your wrists elbows and shoulders should be in line;
2. Centre your head in a neutral position;
3. Gently inhale and exhale for a count of five as you feel your Solar Plexus Chakra glowing, expanding and pulsating.

Cat Pose

1. Start on your hands and knees with your back flat in a table-top position, making sure your knees are directly below your hips. Your wrists, elbows and shoulders should be in line (as with the Cow Pose). Gently draw lower tummy muscles towards spine;

2. Centre your head in a neutral position;

3. As you exhale, round your spine toward the ceiling, making sure you keep your shoulders and knees in position. Release your head towards the floor (do not force your chin to your chest);

4. Inhale coming back to the neutral table-top position;

5. Repeat five times as you visualise a brilliant yellow disc in your Solar Plexus Chakra area, vibrating, pulsating and expanding.

NB: The Cat Pose and the Cow Pose flow together. When combining the poses focus on the breath, noting that the breath flows out as you arch your back and breathe in as you curve back down with buttocks and head up. Be sure to do this slowly, not fast.

Other Activities to Activate and Maintain Your Flow in the Solar Plexus Chakra

Clothing – Wearing yellow clothing and accessories can help stimulate your Solar Plexus Chakra. Have fun with this! I will often have a coloured day, depending on the chakra I am working with at the time.

Try new things – Do at least one new thing each day, it doesn't matter how small; cook something new, listen to an alternate style of music or drive an alternate route to work. The aim is to get comfortable trying new things.

Spend time in the sun – wear sun protection and a sun hat.

Clean up – Tidy your environment, clear clutter, and honour your space.

Create to do lists – Working through daily to do lists will set the scene for setting and achieving larger goals.

Start making decisions – Get comfortable making decisions for yourself and those around you. Start with little things like where to go for dinner or what movie to watch.

Meditations – Meditations are useful for connecting with your higher self and allowing yourself space and time to reflect. If you have never meditated you do not have to be a Zen Monk to practice the art of meditation; you can simply follow along with a guided meditation and take the time out to focus your intentions. There are many guided meditations available for use.

The Chakra Mindset meditations have a short meditation of up to fifteen minutes for each chakra. Take the time each day to complete the meditation relevant to the chakra you are working with.

Chapter 6

Getting to Know Your Chakras – Heart Chakra

Heart Chakra Summary Chart

Names	Heart Chakra, Anaharta
Symbol	Lotus flower with twelve petals
Location	Centre of the chest, sternum
Element	Air
Sense	Touch
Plane	Balance
Colour	Green
Ruling Planet	Venus

The Heart Chakra is the centre of love and gratitude. It is located in the centre of the chest on the sternum. It is our place of compassion, inner peace and understanding; a place of genuine acceptance for self, others and the world around us.

The heart centre is often associated with healing and referred to as the place of healing. When we truly follow our heart it has positive effects across many aspects of our lives.

Balanced Heart Chakra

When you have a balanced Heart Chakra you give and receive love and affection effortlessly. You have compassion and are non-judgemental. You live a life of gratitude and accept people for who they are.

You will have a relaxed, easy approach to relationships and you enjoy time with others as well as time to yourself. If you are in a relationship you will have a mutual respect and understanding of your partner. If you are single you will have a good sense of self and be happy in the knowledge that if you did want a relationship, you would wait for the right person to come along and not feel the need to rush. You follow your heart and it leads you wisely.

Underactive Heart Chakra

When your Heart Chakra is underactive you may find it difficult to open up and let others get close, you may lack empathy and can appear to be cold and insensitive. Your posture may be poor with rounded shoulders and sunken looking chest.

You may feel unlovable and rejected. You fear social situations and are hesitant to get into relationships for fear of rejection or getting hurt. Your love of self is as restricted as your love of others.

Overactive Heart Chakra

An overactive Heart Chakra can manifest in clingy, overbearing behaviour. You may spend all of your time giving to others, putting their needs first, and in giving so much you start to feel resentment in the giving, and may demonstrate a martyr type of attitude.

You may be ruled by your emotions and be overly judgemental of yourself and others.

NB: Some symptoms of an overactive and underactive chakra can be similar, or interchangeable. Simply read each of the patterns to see what you relate to. When we are working on increasing the energy flow in any area, remember it is OK to increase positive energy, even if you feel you may have the symptoms of an overactive chakra. The positive energy will reverse the impact of the overactive negative energy, because it is coming from a place of thriving rather than a place of just surviving.

Physical Issues of an Unbalanced Heart Chakra

The Heart Chakra governs our heart, circulatory system, lungs, ribcage, breasts and blood pressure.

Some of the physical indicators of an unbalanced Heart Chakra may include:

85

- Breast problems
- Breathing disorders and infections
- Painful arms and hands
- Allergies
- Immune system disorders
- Circulation problems
- High blood pressure
- Sleep disturbances

The Parts that Make the Whole

The symbol for the Heart Chakra is a lotus with twelve petals. The parts that make up the Heart Chakra correspond to the number of petals, or can be half of that, which is six, if you are starting out on your journey. Or it may be as many parts as you feel are required for your ideal flow in the Heart Chakra. Expanding on the number of parts is recommended once you have become familiar with the Chakra Mindset concept.

Limiting Beliefs

The list below provides some examples of limiting beliefs that could cause your Heart Chakra to not function at its best:

- I am not loveable
- I do not trust

- I do not love
- I am unworthy
- I am ugly
- I am unlovable
- I am not good enough
- I can only trust myself
- If I don't let anyone close, I cannot get hurt
- Expressing my emotions only leads to heartache

Goal Setting – SMART Goal Example

As part of the goal setting process the following is an example of a SMART goal.

Part – I Feel

Mini Goal – I will spend the week getting in touch with my feelings by writing about them in my journal each day.

Journal

Focused Intention Technique

Decide on up to three states you would like to stack as part of your process for creating your Heart Chakra Point. Use your parts as inspiration for these states.

An example of how to use parts chosen to develop your Heart Chakra Point is as follows:

Three of the parts that you may have chosen to work on in the Heart Chakra:

- Forgiving
- Deserving
- Empathetic

An example of states to use to reinforce these parts may be to recall a time when:

- You forgave someone and were able to move on
- You felt deserving to receive
- You felt real empathy

We are looking for distinct, separate occasions for each state you would like to stack. If you cannot recall a time when you felt what you would like to achieve, I would like you to imagine what it would feel like. Do try to recall a natural state in the first instance as this is far more effective. Write your three states in your

Journal

Activities to Balance Your Heart Chakra

Morning Moments – The practice of morning moments gives you a great start to the day and takes minimal time to complete.

The entire process takes under five minutes. Morning moments are a combination of your gratitude practice, your mantras and visualisations.

Gratitude Practice –A gratitude practice is the practice of taking some time each day to list what you are grateful for. In relation to your Heart Chakra, some of the things you may choose to be grateful for may include:

- Your relationships
- Your generosity
- Your empathy
- Yourself
- Being alive
- Your ability to feel
- Your ability to forgive
- Your ability to see the best in situations
- Your compassion

This simple practice of gratitude gives you the space to stop and appreciate what you have. Gratitude will attract more things in your life to be grateful for. A good practice to get into either first thing in the morning or last thing before you go to bed is to simply acknowledge and be grateful for the things you have.

Another great way of doing this is to keep a picture of all the things you are grateful for. You may want to start by taking one photo a day; spend some time reflecting and looking over these pictures. The more you look for things to be grateful for the more you will find.

Mantras – Creating mantras that you can repeat daily either as part of your morning moments or meditation process is a powerful and effective method of bringing your desired intentions into reality.

A good way to create mantras is to use your chosen chakra parts, and insert an 'I am', or an 'I' in front of the phrase. For example:

- Understanding – I am understanding
- Forgiving – I forgive
- Accepting – I accept
- Trusting – I trust

Visualising your ideal day – Take the time to visualise, feel and create your ideal day. Imagine feeling and seeing your interactions with others, your results, and how you would like the events of the day to play out.

Essential Oils

Essential oils have been used for thousands of years to treat both mental and physical conditions; there are various essential oils that are recommended for each of the chakras.

Some of the uses for essential oils may include:

- Aromatherapy – diffusing oils
- Essential oil baths
- Essential oil massages
- Essential oil creams
- Essential oil mists

Some therapeutic grade essential oils can be applied directly to the skin and some high grade therapeutic essential oils can even be ingested; however, you would need to confirm with the manufacturer the grade and quality of the oils, as well as confirm the recommended uses.

You could experiment by combining two or three of the recommended essential oils into a carrier cream and use the cream as hand moisturiser whilst you are working with the Heart Chakra.

Essential oils that are particularly good when working with the Heart Chakra include:

- Rose
- Benzoin
- Carnation
- Eucalyptus
- Chamomile
- Peppermint

You may find other oils that stimulate your Heart Chakra. Go towards scents that you feel are inviting, loving and uplifting.

Crystals

The use of crystals as healing and divination tools goes back centuries; crystals can be used for meditation, healing, reflection, or simply as an ornament to beautify a space or a piece of jewellery. Crystals can absorb and transmute negative energy and are great to use when you are focusing on your chakras.

Some of the uses for crystals when working with the chakras may include:

- Meditation
- Carrying the crystal in a bag or pocket
- Wearing the crystal in a piece of jewellery
- Keeping the crystals in your environment
- Crystal therapy – You may wish to see a practitioner for a crystal chakra balance. You will find most alternate therapists can assist with this service

Different crystals have different healing attributes. Some of the crystals recommended when working with your Heart Chakra include:

- Jade
- Emerald
- Rose Quartz
- Malachite
- Amazonite

You may be drawn to other crystals when you are working with your Heart Chakra. Trust your instincts. You may find other crystals that are predominately green or pink in colour that you may choose to work with.

Physical Exercises

The following is a list of exercises you may wish to choose from when working on your Heart Chakra. Like any physical program you should consult your doctor before starting a new regime.

Some exercises recommended specifically for the Heart Chakra include:

- Yoga
- Aerobic exercises
- Any exercise that makes you feel good

Yoga Poses

Yoga poses recommended for working on your Heart Chakra, include the Alternate Nostril Breath and the Triangle Pose.

Alternate Nostril Breath

1. Begin in the easy pose sitting with legs crossed, your knees wide and each foot beneath the opposite knee, with your hands resting gently on your knees. Make sure that your weight is even across your buttocks;

2. Close your right nostril with your right thumb and inhale through your left nostril for a count of three;

3. Use your little finger of your right hand to close your left nostril and release your right thumb exhaling through your right nostril;

4. Repeat for a total of three times on each side.

Triangle Pose

1. Triangle Pose begins in the mountain pose; take a step out extending your legs wider than shoulder span, toes pointing forward;

2. Inhale and turn right foot towards the right;

3. Keep feet and hips parallel raising arms sideways to shoulder height, palms facing downwards;

4. Exhale and bend sideways from the waist, down to the right, reaching the left arm upwards, palm turned out to the front, look up at your left hand (only lean out as far as comfortable towards the ground, do not force or stretch the movement);

5. Come back to the start position and change sides raising your right arm up to the ceiling, repeat three times on either side.

NB: This pose should be avoided if you have a back injury.

Other Activities to Activate and Maintain Your Flow in the Heart Chakra

Clothing – Wearing green or pink clothing and accessories can help stimulate your Heart Chakra. Have fun with this! I will often have a coloured day, depending on the chakra I am working with at the time.

Donate your time to a charity – Allow yourself to experience the joy of giving with no expectations.

Practice forgiveness – Make time to let go of any ill feeling you may have towards yourself and/or others.

Mirror gazing – Look at yourself and practice saying I love you.

Have a massage – Allow yourself to enjoy being nurtured.

Meditations – Meditations are useful for connecting with your higher self and allowing yourself space and time to reflect. If you have never meditated you do not have to be a Zen Monk to practice the art of meditation; you can simply follow along with a guided meditation and take the time out to focus your intentions. There are many guided meditations available for use.

The Chakra Mindset meditations have a short meditation of up to fifteen minutes for each chakra. Take the time each day to complete the meditation relevant to the chakra you are working with.

Chapter 7

Getting to Know Your Chakras – Throat Chakra

Throat Chakra Summary Chart

Names	Throat Chakra, Vishuddha
Symbol	Lotus flower with sixteen petals
Location	Throat
Element	Akasha
Sense	Hearing
Plane	Human plane
Colour	Blue
Ruling Planet	Jupiter

The Throat Chakra is the centre of communication; it's about speaking out, and having the ability to speak our truth about any and all things. It is located in the throat. It is also about listening as well as speaking, it governs our willingness to listen to both external and internal things.

The throat centre is also associated with self-expression, allowing us to bring our feelings, thoughts and ideas to others instead of keeping them repressed for fear of judgement or ridicule. The Throat Chakra is also connected to artistic expression of self through art, music, or dance.

Balanced Throat Chakra

When you have a balanced Throat Chakra you are comfortable with self-expression. You are a good communicator, happy to share your ideas and thoughts with others.

You will have a confident and comfortable approach to all areas of communication. You are a great listener, who has the ability to really get what people are saying by listening to what is meant as well as the words used.

You are creative and are able to express yourself through your hobbies and/or chosen career.

Underactive Throat Chakra

When your Throat Chakra is underactive you may find it difficult to speak up and tell others how you really feel. You put others feelings before your own and may be dishonest in order to be liked or to keep the peace. You are afraid of judgement, and keep your opinions to yourself.

You may feel victimised and keep your feelings repressed as a result of feeling inadequate and afraid of judgement.

Overactive Throat Chakra

An overactive Throat Chakra can manifest in being overbearing, in forcing your opinion and thoughts down other's throats. You may notice that you are a poor listener and speak out of turn with little to no regard for others.

NB: Some symptoms of an overactive and underactive chakra can be similar, or interchangeable, simply read each of the patterns to see what you relate to. When we are working on increasing the energy flow in any area, remember it is OK to increase positive energy, even if you feel you may have the symptoms of an overactive chakra. The positive energy will reverse the impact of the overactive negative energy, because it is coming from a place of thriving rather than a place of just surviving.

Physical Issues of an Unbalanced Throat Chakra

The Throat Chakra governs our throat, neck, mouth, teeth, gums, thyroid and cervical spine.

Some of the physical indicators of an unbalanced Throat Chakra may include:

 Ear infections
 Tonsillitis
 Laryngitis

- Thyroid problems
- Hay fever
- Stutter
- Neck and shoulder problems
- Teeth and dental problems

The Parts that Make the Whole

The symbol for the Throat Chakra is a lotus with sixteen petals. The parts that make up the Throat Chakra correspond to the number of petals, or can be half of that, which is eight, if you are starting out on your journey. Or it may be as many parts as you feel are required for your ideal flow in the Throat Chakra. Expanding on the number of parts is recommended once you have become familiar with the Chakra Mindset concept.

Limiting Beliefs

The list below provides some examples of limiting beliefs that could cause your Throat Chakra to not function at its best:

- I am not qualified enough to share my thoughts
- I do not trust
- I am not loved
- I am always rejected
- I am unworthy
- I am stupid

- I am not worth listening to
- I am not good enough
- No one would believe me
- Don't tell people how you feel, they only hurt you
- I am a bad speaker
- I am scared of public speaking

Goal Setting - SMART Goal Example

As part of the goal setting process the following is an example of a SMART goal.

Part – Good Listener

Mini Goal – I will ensure that I listen to people attentively this week, I will do this by being present, and asking appropriate questions.

Journal

Focused Intention Technique

Decide on up to three states you would like to stack as part of your process for creating your Throat Chakra Point. Use your parts as inspiration for these states.

An example of how to use parts chosen to develop your Throat Chakra Point is as follows:

Three of the parts that you may have chosen to work on in the Throat Chakra:

✸ Safe

✸ Good Communicator

✸ Speak the Truth

An example of states to use to reinforce these parts may be to recall a time when:

✸ You felt totally safe

✸ You communicated really well, and people understood what you were saying

✸ You spoke your truth and it was OK

We are looking for distinct separate occasions for each state you would like to stack. If you cannot recall a time when you felt what you would like to achieve, I would like you to imagine what it would feel like. Do try to recall a natural state in the first instance as this is far more effective. Write your three states in your *Journal*

Activities to Balance Your Throat Chakra

Morning Moments – The practice of morning moments gives you a great start to the day and takes minimal time to complete. The entire process takes under five minutes. Morning moments are a combination of your gratitude practice, your mantras and visualisations.

Gratitude Practice – A gratitude practice is the practice of taking some time each day to list what you are grateful for. In relation to your Throat Chakra, some of the things you may choose to be grateful for may include:

* Your voice
* Your creativity
* Your empathy
* Yourself
* Being alive
* Your ability to tell a story
* Your ability to listen
* Your ability to let others shine
* Your compassion
* Freedom of speech

This simple practice of gratitude gives you the space to stop and appreciate what you have. Gratitude will attract more things in your life to be grateful for. A good practice to get into either first thing in the morning or last thing before you go to bed is to simply acknowledge and be grateful for the things you have.

Another great way of doing this is to keep a picture of all the things you are grateful for. You may want to start by taking one photo a day; spend some time reflecting and looking over these pictures. The more you look for things to be grateful for the more you will find.

Mantras – Creating mantras that you can repeat daily either as part of your morning moments or meditation process is a powerful and effective method of bringing your desired intentions into reality.

A good way to create mantras is to use your chosen chakra parts, and insert an 'I am', or an 'I' in front of the phrase. For example:

- Good Listener – I am a good listener
- Powerful – I am powerful
- Safe – I am safe
- Centred – I am centred

Visualising your ideal day – Take the time to visualise, feel and create your ideal day. Imagine feeling and seeing your interactions with others, your results, and how you would like the events of the day to play out.

Essential Oils

Essential oils have been used for thousands of years to treat both mental and physical conditions; there are various essential oils that are recommended for each of the chakras.

Some of the uses for essential oils may include:

- Aromatherapy – diffusing oils
- Essential oil baths

❋ Essential oil massages
❋ Essential oil creams
❋ Essential oil mists

Some therapeutic grade essential oils can be applied directly to the skin and some high grade therapeutic essential oils can even be ingested; however, you would need to confirm with the manufacturer the grade and quality of the oils as well as confirm the recommended uses.

You could experiment by combining two or three of the recommended essential oils into a carrier cream and use the cream as hand moisturiser whilst you are working with the Throat Chakra.

Essential oils that are particularly good when working with the Throat Chakra include:

❋ Ylang Ylang
❋ Blue Chamomile
❋ Patchouli
❋ Blue Tansy

You may find other oils that stimulate your Throat Chakra. Go towards scents that you feel are expressive.

Crystals

The use of crystals as healing and divination tools goes back centuries; crystals can be used for meditation, healing, reflection, or simply as an ornament to beautify a space or a piece of jewellery. Crystals can absorb and transmute negative energy and are great to use when you are focusing on your chakras.

Some of the uses for crystals when working with the chakras may include:

- Meditation
- Carrying the crystal in a bag or pocket
- Wearing the crystal in a piece of jewellery
- Keeping the crystals in your environment
- Crystal therapy – You may wish to see a practitioner for a crystal chakra balance. You will find most alternate therapists can assist with this service

Different crystals have different healing attributes. Some of the crystals recommended when working with your Throat Chakra include:

- Aquamarine
- Blue Agate
- Blue Calcite
- Turquoise
- Angelite

You may be drawn to other crystals when you are working with your Throat Chakra, trust your instincts. You may find other crystals that are predominately blue in colour that you may choose to work with.

Physical Exercises

The following is a list of exercises you may wish to choose from when working on your Throat Chakra. Like any physical program you should consult your doctor before starting a new regime.

Some exercises recommended specifically for the Throat Chakra include:

* Yoga
* Dance
* Tai Chi
* Any exercise that allows you to express yourself

Yoga Poses

Yoga Poses recommended for working on your Throat Chakra, include the Lion's Pose and Chin Lock.

Lion's Pose

1. Kneel on the floor with your hands comfortably by your side, and sit back on your heels (you may wish to use a small cushion under your knees for greater comfort);

2. Lean forward and place both hands flat on the ground in front of your knees, about two hands span away from your knees;

3. Open your mouth wide, stretching your tongue out as far as possible, whilst making an "ah" sound (don't be shy, make sure the sound is audible);

4. Repeat three times and relax.

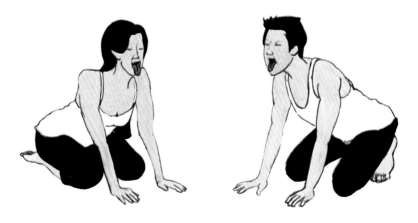

Chin Lock

1. Sit in a half lotus position (as per diagram on page 142 lotus pose);

2. Inhale and slowly lower your head down to your chest, hold your breath about 30 seconds;

Raise your head up and exhale, repeat three times.

Other Activities to Activate and Maintain Your Flow in the Throat Chakra

Clothing – Wearing blue clothing and accessories can help stimulate your Throat Chakra. Have fun with this! I will often have a coloured day, depending on the chakra I am working with at the time.

Read out loud – Get used to hearing your own voice.

Sing – Sing out loud, no matter who can hear.

Creative writing – Take some time out to write about anything that brings you joy, you may wish to write some poetry.

Meditations – Meditations are useful for connecting with your higher self and allowing yourself space and time to reflect. If you have never meditated you do not have to be a Zen Monk to practice the art of meditation; you can simply follow along with a guided meditation and take the time out to focus your intentions. There are many guided meditations available for use.

The Chakra Mindset meditations have a short meditation of up to fifteen minutes for each chakra. Take the time each day to complete the meditation relevant to the chakra you are working with.

Chapter 8

Getting to Know Your Chakras – Third Eye Chakra

Third Eye Chakra Summary Chart

Names	Third Eye Chakra, Ajna
Symbol	Lotus flower with two petals
Location	Centre of forehead
Element	Mahat
Sense	Sixth sense
Plane	Austerity
Colour	Indigo
Ruling Planet	Saturn

The Third Eye Chakra is the centre of intuition and insight. It is located in the centre of the forehead. This chakra determines your ability to trust and interpret your ability to see what is, and visualise what could be. The Third Eye Chakra governs your depth of foresight and knowing. It allows you to expand your awareness to encompass all possibilities. Your comfort in this chakra is gained when you trust and allow yourself to see and manifest without fear of failure, judgement or consequence.

The Third Eye Chakra is also connected to imagination, wisdom and intellect.

Balanced Third Eye Chakra

When you have a balanced Third Eye Chakra you have an active imagination, you are comfortable with visualising your desired outcomes and you trust your intuition.

You will have a comfortable balance between the ability to analyse the facts, measure the consequences, and trust in your ability to manifest based on your visualisation and clarity of purpose. You have great focus and are able to concentrate your energy on the desired outcomes. You have good dream recall and are open to exploring what they mean to you.

Underactive Third Eye Chakra

When your Third Eye Chakra is underactive you may find it difficult to use your imagination, you may notice that your ability to focus and visualise your goals is diminished. This may be demonstrated through the inability to set your mind to a task and follow through. This is because you do not connect with the possibilities and allow yourself to see the outcome.

You may have poor dream recall and shy away from your intuitive thoughts and feelings.

Overactive Third Eye Chakra

An overactive Third Eye Chakra can manifest in being unrealistic, with your head up in the clouds, with little to no connection with reality. You may tend to fantasise and not be able to distinguish between the physical realm and that of illusion, and may exhibit delusional thoughts and/or behaviours.

NB: Some symptoms of an overactive and underactive chakra can be similar, or interchangeable, simply read each of the patterns to see what you relate to. When we are working on increasing the energy flow in any area, remember it is OK to increase positive energy, even if you feel you may have the symptoms of an overactive chakra. The positive energy will reverse the impact of the overactive negative energy, because it is coming from a place of thriving rather than a place of just surviving.

Physical Issues of an Unbalanced Third Eye Chakra

The Third Eye Chakra governs our vision, sinus, head, and pituitary gland.

Some of the physical indicators of an unbalanced Third Eye Chakra may include:

- Headaches
- Allergies
- Eye problems

- Vertigo
- Anxiety disorders
- Neurological problems
- Body image disorders
- Sinus and nose problems
- Hormone problems
- Ear infections
- Insomnia

The Parts that Make the Whole

The symbol for the Third Eye Chakra is a lotus with two large petals comprising of forty-eight smaller petals per large petal. The parts that make up the Third Eye Chakra is two; corresponding to the number of petals. Or it may be as many parts as you feel are required for your ideal flow in the Third Eye Chakra. Expanding on the number of parts is recommended once you have become familiar with the Chakra Mindset concept.

Limiting Beliefs

The list below provides some examples of limiting beliefs that could cause your Third Eye Chakra to not function at its best:

- I do not trust myself
- I am scared to see the future

- I am making it up
- I am afraid to open myself up as it will hurt me
- I am unworthy
- I am blind
- I do not deserve to see my full potential
- I am not good enough
- No one would believe me
- Don't tell people about the possibilities, they will ridicule me
- I have no clarity, because I am stupid
- I can't focus long enough to see the possibilities

Goal Setting – SMART Goal Example

As part of the goal setting process the following is an example of a SMART goal.

Part – Focused

Mini Goal – I will be 100% focused on working through my action plan this week. I will set time aside time in my diary to complete all activities and meditations.

Journal

Focused Intention Technique

Decide on up to three states you would like to stack as part of your process for creating your Third Eye Chakra Point. Use your parts as inspiration for these states.

An example of how to use parts chosen to develop your Third Eye Chakra Point is as follows:

Three of the parts that you may have chosen to work on in the Third Eye Chakra:

-  Purposeful
- Seek out Opportunity
- Intuitive

An example of states to use to reinforce these parts may be to recall a time when:

- You felt right on purpose, and worked towards an outcome
- You took the time to seek out an opportunity and followed through
- You trusted your intuition and it served you well

We are looking for distinct, separate occasions for each state you would like to stack. If you cannot recall a time when you felt what you would like to achieve, I would like you to imagine what it would feel like. Do try to recall a natural state in the first instance as this is far more effective. Write your three states in your *Journal*

Activities to Balance your Third Eye Chakra

Morning Moments – The practice of morning moments gives you a great start to the day and takes minimal time to complete. The entire process takes under five minutes. Morning moments are a combination of your gratitude practice, your mantras and visualisations.

Gratitude Practice – A gratitude practice is the practice of taking some time each day to list what you are grateful for. In relation to your Third Eye Chakra, some of the things you may choose to be grateful for may include:

- Your imagination
- Your ability to visualise
- Your focus
- Your attention to detail
- Being alive
- Your ability to see into the future
- Your ability to trust yourself
- Your creativity
- Your wisdom
- The beauty around you

This simple practice of gratitude gives you the space to stop and appreciate what you have. Gratitude will attract more things in your life to be grateful for. A good practice to get into either first thing in the morning or last thing before you go to bed is to simply acknowledge and be grateful for the things you have.

Another great way of doing this is to keep a picture of all the things you are grateful for. You may want to start by taking one photo a day; spend some time reflecting and looking over these pictures. The more you look for things to be grateful for the more you will find.

Mantras – Creating mantras that you can repeat daily either as part of your morning moments or meditation process is a powerful and effective method of bringing your desired intentions into reality.

A good way to create mantras is to use your chosen chakra parts, and insert an 'I am', or an 'I' in front of the phrase. For example:

- Intuitive – I am intuitive
- Wise – I am wise
- Imaginative – I am imaginative
- Insightful – I am insightful

Visualising your ideal day – Take the time to visualise, feel and create your ideal day. Imagine feeling and seeing your interactions with others, your results, and how you would like the events of the day to play out.

Essential Oils

Essential oils have been used for thousands of years to treat both mental and physical conditions; there are various essential oils that are recommended for each of the chakras.

Some of the uses for essential oils may include:

- Aromatherapy – diffusing oils
- Essential oil baths
- Essential oil massages
- Essential oil creams
- Essential oil mists

Some therapeutic grade essential oils can be applied directly to the skin and some high grade therapeutic essential oils can even be ingested; however, you would need to confirm with the manufacturer the grade and quality of the oils, as well as confirm the recommended uses.

You could experiment by combining two or three of the recommended essential oils into a carrier cream and use the cream as hand moisturiser whilst you are working with the Third Eye Chakra.

Essential oils that are particularly good when working with the Third Eye Chakra include:

- Rosemary
- Clary Sage

- Juniper
- Peppermint
- Geranium

You may find other oils that stimulate your Third Eye Chakra. Go towards scents that you feel allow you to tap into your imagination.

Crystals

The use of crystals as healing and divination tools goes back centuries; crystals can be used for meditation, healing, reflection, or simply as an ornament to beautify a space or a piece of jewellery. Crystals can absorb and transmute negative energy and are great to use when you are focusing on your chakras.

Some of the uses for crystals when working with the chakras may include:

- Meditation
- Carrying the crystal in a bag or pocket
- Wearing the crystal in a piece of jewellery
- Keeping the crystals in your environment
- Crystal therapy – You may wish to see a practitioner for a crystal chakra balance. You will find most alternate therapists can assist with this service

Different crystals have different healing attributes. Some of the crystals recommended when working with your Third Eye Chakra include:

◉ Amethyst
◉ Lapis Lazuli
◉ Quartz
◉ Azurite
◉ Moonstone

You may be drawn to other crystals when you are working with your Third Eye Chakra, trust your instincts. You may find other crystals that are predominately indigo or clear in colour that you may choose to work with.

Physical Exercises

Your Third Eye Chakra is the centre for intuition and visualisation, any type of exercise that requires focus would be a great inclusion to your daily program when working with the Third Eye Chakra. Like any physical program you should consult your doctor before starting a new regime.

Some exercises recommended specifically for the Third Eye Chakra include:

◉ Yoga
◉ Archery
◉ Darts
◉ Orienteering

Yoga Poses

Yoga Poses recommended for working on your Third Eye Chakra, include the Child's Pose and the Downward Dog.

Child's Pose

1. Get into a kneeling position and then sit back on your heels;

2. Bend forward bringing the torso over the thighs and your forehead to the ground, arms stretched out in front of you, hands flat on the ground;

3. Relax into the ground and hold for a count of three to five breaths.

Downward Dog Pose

1. Get on your hands and knees, hands beneath your shoulders and knees beneath hips;

2. Curl your toes under and press the balls of your feet to the ground;

3. Lift your hips towards the ceiling until your body makes an inverted V shape;

4. Keep your eyes focused on your feet, your chest towards your knees and your head in between your arms towards the floor;

5. Hold for a count of three to five breaths.

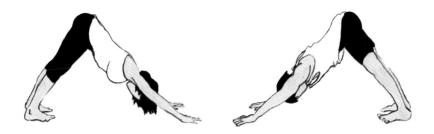

Other Activities to Activate and Maintain Your Flow in the Third Eye Chakra

Clothing – Wearing indigo clothing and accessories can help stimulate your Third Eye Chakra. Have fun with this! I will often have a coloured day, depending on the chakra I am working with at the time.

Do visualisation exercises – Practice using your imagination to visualise and create images in your mind's eye.

Dream Journal – Keep a dream journal by your bed so that you can capture your dreams as soon as you wake to improve dream recall.

Meditations – Meditations are useful for connecting with your higher self and allowing yourself space and time to reflect. If you have never meditated you do not have to be a Zen Monk to practice the art of meditation; you can simply follow along with a guided meditation and take the time out to focus your intentions. There are many guided meditations available for use.

The Chakra Mindset meditations have a short meditation of up to fifteen minutes for each chakra. Take the time each day to complete the meditation relevant to the chakra you are working with.

Chapter 9

Getting to Know Your Chakras – Crown Chakra

Crown Chakra Summary Chart

Names	Crown Chakra, Sahasrara
Symbol	Lotus flower with one thousand petals
Location	Top of head
Element	None
Sense	None
Plane	Truth
Colour	Violet to clear with all colours of the rainbow
Ruling Planet	Ketu

The Crown Chakra is located on the top of your head. It is your connection to source, whatever that may be for you. It is the place of universal consciousness, where we gain the understanding that we are more than just our physical selves. Regardless of religion, spiritual belief or upbringing, the Crown Chakra extends and connects us to all things. It rules our ability and beliefs around expansion and service to others. Here we lose sense of our individual identity and become one with all. Judgement, ego and fear are released and a state of self-actualisation is achieved.

The Crown Chakra is nirvana. It is all things.

Balanced Crown Chakra

When you have a balanced Crown Chakra you will be ruled by pure joy and a desire to be of service. You are not driven by ego or materialistic gain. You are connected to a multidimensional consciousness and have empathy for all people and all things; your desire for unity and the good of all is omnipresent. You are one with the divine.

Underactive Crown Chakra

When your Crown Chakra is underactive you struggle with making decisions. You may be very one minded when it comes to spirituality and cynical when it comes to the belief systems of others. Your life lacks joy and vitality; never feeling satisfied or content, and always searching for that missing piece of the puzzle. You drift from day to day with no real sense of purpose or meaning.

Overactive Crown Chakra

You can be egotistical and domineering. Your beliefs systems are rigid and inflexible; you only see one point of view, your own. Alternatively an overactive Crown Chakra can manifest a delusional fantasised view of the world and your place in it. Your feeling of superiority is demonstrated through your lack of concern or empathy for universal issues, with little to no consideration for life beyond your own.

NB: Some symptoms of an overactive and underactive chakra can be similar, or interchangeable. Simply read each of the patterns to see what you relate to. When we are working on increasing the energy flow in any area, remember it is ok to increase positive energy, even if you feel you may have the symptoms of an overactive chakra. The positive energy will reverse the impact of the overactive negative energy, because it is coming from a place of thriving rather than a place of just surviving.

Physical Issues of an Unbalanced Crown Chakra

The Crown Chakra governs our lymphatic system, skull and brain.

Some of the physical indicators of an unbalanced Crown Chakra may include:

- Depression
- Sensitivity to light and sound
- Learning difficulties
- Schizophrenia
- Migraine headaches
- Insomnia

- Epilepsy
- Psychosis
- Dizziness

The Parts that Make the Whole

The symbol for the Crown Chakra is a lotus with a thousand petals. The parts that make up the Crown Chakra are infinite, therefore left to each individual to determine. If you are new to the Chakra Mindset concept I recommend starting with one or two parts, and if you are experienced in working with the chakras you can have as many parts as you feel make up your ideal flow in the Crown Chakra.

Limiting Beliefs

The list below provides some examples of limiting beliefs that could cause your Crown Chakra to not function at its best:

- I am alone
- There is no God, greater power, creator, etc.
- This is life, what you see is what you get
- I am not worthy
- If I care for others they only disappoint me
- It's survival of the fittest, I put myself first always
- I have no clarity, because I was brought up with no real direction
- I cannot choose my beliefs. I must take on those of my family

Goal Setting – SMART Goal Example

As part of the goal setting process the following is an example of a SMART goal.

Part – Purpose

Mini Goal – I will take one hour on Wednesday of this week to reflect upon and write down what I believe my life purpose to be. In order to gain a better understanding of this I will ask myself the following questions:

What do I think my purpose is?

When will I take some action towards living my purpose?

Why is my purpose what I have decided on?

How will I continue to work towards it?

Journal

Focused Intention Technique

Decide on up to three states you would like to stack as part of your process for creating your Crown Chakra Point. Use your parts as inspiration for these states.

An example of how to use parts chosen to develop your Crown Chakra Point is as follows:

Two of the parts that you may have chosen to work on in the Crown Chakra:

- Inspired
- Connected

An example of states to use to reinforce these parts may be to recall a time when:

- You felt truly inspired
- You felt really connected

We are looking for distinct, separate occasions for each state you would like to stack. If you cannot recall a time when you felt what you would like to achieve, I would like you to imagine what it would feel like. Do try to recall a natural state in the first instance as this is far more effective. Write your three states in your *Journal*

Activities to Balance Your Crown Chakra

Morning Moments – The practice of morning moments gives you a great start to the day and takes minimal time to complete. The entire process takes under five minutes. Morning moments are a combination of your gratitude practice, your mantras and visualisations.

Gratitude Practice – A gratitude practice is the practice of taking some time each day to list what you are grateful for. In relation to your Crown Chakra, some of the things you may choose to be grateful for may include:

- Your beliefs
- Your connection to others
- The world you live in
- The good in others
- The inspiration you find all around you
- Your freedom of choice
- Life
- Others
- The creator, the one, the universe

This simple practice of gratitude gives you the space to stop and appreciate what you have. Gratitude will attract more things in your life to be grateful for. A good practice to get into either first thing in the morning or last thing before you go to bed is to simply acknowledge and be grateful for the things you have.

Another great way of doing this is to keep a picture of all the things you are grateful for. You may want to start by taking one photo a day; spend some time reflecting and looking over these pictures. The more you look for things to be grateful for the more you will find.

Mantras – Creating mantras that you can repeat daily either as part of your morning moments or meditation process is a powerful and effective method of bringing your desired intentions into reality.

A good way to create mantras is to use your chosen chakra parts, and insert an 'I am', or an 'I' in front of the phrase. For example:

- Spiritual – I am spiritual
- Consciousness – I am conscious
- Pure bliss – I am pure bliss
- Knowing – I am knowing

Visualising your ideal day – Take the time to visualise, feel and create your ideal day. Imagine feeling and seeing your interactions with others, your results, and how you would like the events of the day to play out.

Essential Oils

Essential oils have been used for thousands of years to treat both mental and physical conditions; there are various essential oils that are recommended for each of the chakras.

Some of the uses for essential oils may include:

- Aromatherapy – diffusing oils
- Essential oil baths
- Essential oil massages
- Essential oil creams
- Essential oil mists

Some therapeutic grade essential oils can be applied directly to the skin and some high grade therapeutic essential oils can even be ingested; however, you would need to confirm with the manufacturer the grade and quality of the oils, as well as confirm the recommended uses.

You could experiment by combining two or three of the recommended essential oils into a carrier cream and use the cream as hand moisturiser whilst you are working with the Crown Chakra.

Essential oils that are particularly good when working with the Crown Chakra include:

139

- Frankincense
- Myrrh
- Lavender
- Jasmine
- Ylang Ylang

You may find other oils that stimulate your Crown Chakra. Go towards scents that bring you contentment and joy.

Crystals

The use of crystals as healing and divination tools goes back centuries; crystals can be used for meditation, healing, reflection, or simply as an ornament to beautify a space or a piece of jewellery. Crystals can absorb and transmute negative energy and are great to use when you are focusing on your chakras.

Some of the uses for crystals when working with the chakras may include:

- Meditation
- Carrying the crystal in a bag or pocket
- Wearing the crystal in a piece of jewellery
- Keeping the crystals in your environment
- Crystal therapy – You may wish to see a practitioner for a crystal chakra balance. You will find most alternate therapists can assist with this service

Different crystals have different healing attributes. Some of the crystals recommended when working with your Crown Chakra include:

- Diamond
- Clear Quartz
- Amethyst
- Selenite

You may be drawn to other crystals when you are working with your Crown Chakra, trust your instincts. You may find other crystals that are reflective of all colours that you may choose to work with.

Physical Exercises

The following is a list of exercises you may wish to choose from when working on your Crown Chakra.

Like any physical program you should consult your doctor before starting a new regime.

Some exercises recommended specifically for the Crown Chakra include:

- Yoga
- Mountain climbing
- Hiking

Yoga Poses

Yoga Poses recommended for working on your Crown Chakra, include the Half Lotus Pose and the Shoulder Stand.

Half Lotus Pose

1. Sit upright with your legs stretched out in front of you and your back upright and straight;
2. Place your hands on the ground beside you to keep you stable, bring your right foot up towards your abdomen and place it on the top of your left thigh;
3. Bring your left foot up towards your abdomen and place it on your right thigh;
4. Place your hands gently on your knees with your palms towards the ceiling;
5. Relax and breathe deeply, hold for as long as you feel comfortable focusing on your breath and your current centred state.

Shoulder Stand Pose

1. Lie on your back;
2. Lift both legs at the same time until you feel your hips raise off the floor;
3. Place your hands together at the back of your hips;
4. Hold for as long as you feel comfortable and gently place your hands by your sides and release back to the floor.

NB: This pose should be avoided if you have a bad neck issues.

Other Activities to Activate and Maintain Your Flow in the Crown Chakra

Clothing – Wearing violet, gold, silver, and all colours of the rainbow clothing and accessories can help stimulate your Crown Chakra. Have fun with this! I will often have a coloured day, depending on the chakra I am working with at the time.

Pray – Spend some time alone in prayer.

Volunteering – Volunteer your time to help those less fortunate than yourself.

Make other people feel good – Do a kind deed, say something nice, make another person's day simply for the joy of it, with no expectation or need for thanks or acknowledgement.

Meditations – Meditations are useful for connecting with your higher self and allowing yourself space and time to reflect. If you have never meditated you do not have to be a Zen Monk to practice the art of meditation; you can simply follow along with a guided meditation and take the time out to focus your intentions. There are many guided meditations available for use.

The Chakra Mindset meditations have a short meditation of up to fifteen minutes for each chakra. Take the time each day to complete the meditation relevant to the chakra you are working with.

Chapter 10

Activating the Chakra Mindset

Chakra State Analysis

In order to move forward and identify what area of your life and what chakras you need to spend more time focusing on you need to first identify the chakra state for each chakra, at this stage of the program we refer to the chakra state as your bridge point. Your bridge point is where you are now and reflects the current results you are having in all areas of your life. Working through the Chakra State Analysis will provide you with an opportunity to reflect on all areas of your life, notice what is going well, and gain an understanding of the areas in which you would like to make some changes.

I would recommend starting at the Root Chakra and working through the chakra state charts. This will make your starting point clear and assist you in identifying what's next, developing the individualised action plan that will help you get underway and start the energy moving in the direction of your choice. The beauty of the program is its simplicity and the fact that you decide the rate of flow and the outcomes you are working towards. Remember you have created the chakra state, or at least accepted it. Now you can choose to change it!

When you undertake the Chakra State Analysis you need to go with your instincts. Do not over-analyse your initial responses. For some this may be the first step to challenging your current obstacles.

Chakra State Analysis - Bridge Point

The Chakra State Analysis is a simple process that allows you to explore the current state of each of your chakras, and start to design how you would like your life to be.

Repeat the following process for each of your chakras. There is space in your journal to complete the Chakra State Analysis, or alternatively you can do the Chakra State Analysis online at www.chakramindset.com.

Journal

Root Chakra

Refer to the statement and words in the table below to come up with your chakra state; your bridge point.

Select one statement, one word or one phrase for each part of the Root Chakra that best represents the current status of your Root Chakra. Be honest with yourself and don't overthink what comes up.

As mentioned previously, the parts that make up the Root Chakra can either correspond to the number of petals, which is four, or can be half of that which is two; this is recommended if you are starting out on your journey. It may also be as many parts as you feel are required for your ideal flow in the Root Chakra once you become familiar with the Chakra Mindset concept.

Positive	Part Selected	Shadow Aspect	Part Selected
Belonging	☐	Do not fit in	☐
Abundant	☐	Lacking	☐
Grounded	☐	Flighty	☐
Family connection	☐	No connection to family	☐
Good relationship with food	☐	Bad relationship with food	☐
Good relationship with money	☐	Bad relationship with money	☐

Trust instincts	☐	Question instincts	☐
Connected to nature	☐	No connection to nature	☐
Thriving	☐	Surviving	☐
Blessed	☐	Cursed	☐
Wanted	☐	Unwanted	☐
Worthy	☐	Unworthy	☐
Chosen	☐	Tolerated	☐
Strong	☐	Weak	☐
Healthy	☐	Sick	☐
Powerful	☐	Defeated	☐
Contribution to others / greater good	☐	Self-centred	☐
Accepted	☐	Rejected	☐
Excited	☐	Afraid	☐
Grateful	☐	Resentful	☐
Free	☐	Trapped	☐
Fluid	☐	Stuck	☐
Planned	☐	Mistake	☐
Living my purpose	☐	Working out of obligation	☐
Healthy weight	☐	Unhealthy weight	☐
Fit	☐	Unfit	☐

Have a look at the words and phrases you have selected. If they sit on the positive side of the chart, write them into the petal parts on the diagram provided.

If they fall under the shadow side of the chart look at the corresponding positive side and decide if the phrase or word resonates with you, or is a good indication of how you would like to feel or how you would like your reality to be. If so, replace the shadow phrase or word with the corresponding positive aspect. If not, have a look at the remainder of the words and phrases on the positive side of the chart and select one that resonates with what you would like your reality to be. Once you have selected a positive word or phrase to replace the shadow word or phrase write it in the petal parts provided.

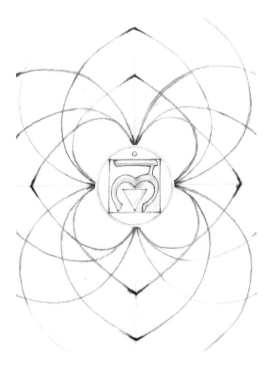

Go through each of your selected parts and rank them from 1 to 10 to gain an understanding of how this part is currently manifesting your reality i.e. if you chose Healthy as a part and you have spent some time working on your health but it is not quite where you would like it to be, you may choose to rank it as a 6.

1 = Long way to go / 10 = I am there.

Use your results from the point above to complete the calculations below in order to find your bridge point.

(a) Root Chakra Bridge Point (total of your selected parts that you have scored out of 10): _____

(b) Possible maximum score of: _____

If you used two petals the maximum score is 20

If you used four petals the maximum score is 40

If you used a number in-between the maximum score is the total of the petals times 10 (petals x 10)

In order to calculate your current bridge point complete the following sum:(a) total of all parts divided by (b) possible maximum score of = _____ Root Chakra Bridge Point

Take some time to reflect. You may like to note in your journal what the current ratings are and have a think about how this is manifesting in your life. Awareness and a will to change are major ingredients required to make positive and lasting change. You may notice if you have any areas with a score above eight, that these are areas in your life that you are getting the results you desire or if not you will be well on the way to having the desired outcome. Areas that scored under eight are the areas that you can focus on to create the energy flow and space required to create momentum to move in the desired direction towards your ideal flow.

If all parts selected exceed a score of 8 out of 10, this would indicate that you are achieving your ideal flow for this particular chakra and may wish to revisit this chakra in the Reinventing Your Ideal Flow chapter, once you have reached your ideal flow in all other areas.

What we will be working towards are rankings of 8 to 10 for all of the parts that form the whole.

You have created movement and have started the energy moving in the direction of your choice in the Root Chakra; you are creating and are within reach of determining the outcome.

Sacral Chakra

Refer to the statement and words in the table below to come up with your chakra state; your bridge point.

Select one statement, one word or one phrase for each part of the Sacral Chakra that best represents the current status of your Sacral Chakra. Be honest with yourself and don't overthink what comes up.

The parts that make up the Sacral Chakra can either correspond to the number of petals, which is six, or can be half of that which is three; this is recommended if you are starting out on your journey. It may also be as many parts as you feel are required for your ideal flow in the Sacral Chakra once you become familiar with the Chakra Mindset concept.

Positive	Part Selected	Shadow Aspect	Part Selected
Pleasure	☐	Pain	☐
Good relationships with others	☐	Bad relationships with others	☐
Sensual	☐	Frigid	☐
Worthy	☐	Unworthy	☐
Good with intimacy	☐	Shy away from intimacy	☐
Playful	☐	Always serious / frigid / stern	☐

Receptive to others	☐	Closed off to others	☐
Lover	☐	Fighter	☐
Noticed	☐	Unnoticed / invisible	☐
Expressive	☐	Withdrawn	☐
Self-nurturing	☐	Self-neglect	☐
Happy	☐	Sad	☐
In control of self	☐	In control of others	☐
Accepted	☐	Rejected	☐
Enjoyment	☐	Obligation	☐
Enjoy sex	☐	Dislike sex	☐
Flowing	☐	Stuck	☐
Creative	☐	Not creative	☐
Excitable	☐	Bored	☐
Free	☐	Trapped	☐
Self-love	☐	Self-hate	☐
Love others	☐	Hate others	☐
Sharing	☐	Selfish	☐
Uninhibited	☐	Self-conscious	☐
Accepting	☐	Rejecting	☐

Have a look at the words and phrases you have selected. If they sit on the positive side of the chart, write them into the petal parts on the diagram provided.

If they fall under the shadow side of the chart look at the corresponding positive side and decide if the phrase or word resonates with you, or is a good indication of how you would like to feel or how you would like your reality to be. If so, replace the shadow phrase or word with the corresponding positive aspect. If not, have a look at the remainder of the words and phrases on the positive side of the chart and select one that resonates with what you would like your reality to be. Once you have selected a positive word or phrase to replace the shadow word or phrase write it in the petal parts provided.

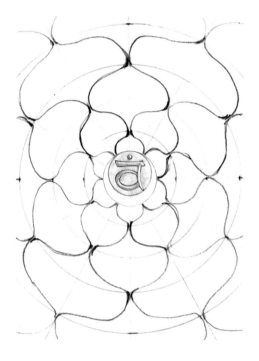

Go through each of your selected parts and rank them from 1 to 10 to gain an understanding of how this part is currently manifesting your reality i.e. if you chose Playful as a part and you find yourself quite serious you may choose to rank it as a 4.

1 = Long way to go / 10 = I am there.

Use your results from the previous point to complete the calculations below in order to find your bridge point.

(a) Sacral Chakra Bridge Point (total of your selected parts that you have scored out of 10): _____

(b) Possible maximum score of: _____

If you used three petals the maximum score is 30

If you used six petals the maximum score is 60

If you used a number in between the maximum score is the total of the petals times 10 (petals x 10)

In order to calculate your current bridge point complete the following sum:(a) total of all parts divided by (b) possible maximum score of = _____ Sacral Chakra Bridge Point

Take some time to reflect. You may like to note in your journal what the current ratings are and have a think about how this is manifesting in your life. Awareness and a will to change are major ingredients required to make positive and lasting change. You may notice if you have any areas with a score above eight, that these are areas in your life that you are getting the results you desire or if not you will be well on the way to having the desired outcome. Areas that scored under eight are the areas that you can focus on to create the energy flow and space required to create momentum to move in the desired direction towards your ideal flow.

If all parts selected exceed a score of 8 out of 10, this would indicate that you are achieving your ideal flow for this particular chakra and may wish to revisit this chakra in the Reinventing Your Ideal Flow chapter, once you have reached your ideal flow in all other areas.

What we will be working towards are rankings of eight to ten for all of the parts that form the whole.

You have created movement and have started the energy moving in the direction of your choice in the Sacral Chakra. You are creating and are within reach of determining the outcome.

Solar Plexus Chakra

Refer to the statement and words in the table below to come up with your chakra state; your bridge point.

Select one statement, one word or one phrase for each part of the Solar Plexus Chakra that best represents the current status of your Solar Plexus Chakra. Be honest with yourself and don't over-think what comes up.

The parts that make up the Solar Plexus Chakra correspond to the number of petals, which is ten, or can be half of that which is five; this is recommended if you are starting out on your journey. It may also be as many parts as you feel are required for your ideal flow in the Solar Plexus Chakra once you become familiar with the Chakra Mindset concept.

Positive	Part Selected	Shadow Aspect	Part Selected
High self-esteem	☐	Low self-esteem	☐
High self-esteem	☐	Grandiose	☐
Willpower	☐	Lack of willpower	☐
Confident	☐	Not confident	☐
Fulfilled	☐	Empty	☐
Accepting	☐	Rejecting	☐
Whole	☐	Empty	☐
Trust intuition	☐	Do not follow intuition	☐

Positive	☐	Negative	☐
Open	☐	Closed	☐
Attractive	☐	Ugly	☐
Strong	☐	Weak	☐
Strong	☐	Overbearing	☐
Powerful	☐	Lack personal power	☐
Powerful	☐	Controlling	☐
Assertive	☐	Aggressive	☐
Assertive	☐	Non-assertive	☐
Visible	☐	Hidden / invisible	☐
Focused	☐	Obsessed	☐
Driven	☐	Lack of drive	☐
Calm	☐	Agitated / stressed	☐
Controlled	☐	No self-control	☐
Happy	☐	Sad	☐
Self-assured	☐	Not confident	☐
Ambitious	☐	No Ambition	☐
Champion	☐	Victim	☐

Have a look at the words and phrases you have selected. If they sit on the positive side of the chart, write them into the petal parts on the diagram provided.

If they fall under the shadow side of the chart look at the corresponding positive side and decide if the phrase or word resonates with you, or is a good indication of how you would like to feel or how you would like your reality to be. If so, replace the shadow phrase or word with the corresponding positive aspect. If not, have a look at the remainder of the words and phrases on the positive side of the chart and select one that resonates with what you would like your reality to be. Once you have selected a positive word or phrase to replace the shadow word or phrase write it in the petal parts provided.

Go through each of your selected parts and rank them from 1 to 10 to gain an understanding of how this part is currently manifesting your reality i.e. if you chose Controlled as a part and you find you're doing well in this area you may rank it as an 8.

1 = Long way to go / 10 = I am there.

Use your results from the previous point to complete the calculations below in order to find your bridge point.

(a) Solar Plexus Chakra Bridge Point (total of your selected parts that you have scored out of 10):_____

(b) Possible maximum score of:_____

If you used five petals the maximum score is 50

If you used ten petals the maximum score is 100

If you used a number in-between the maximum score is the total of the petals times 10 (petals x 10)

In order to calculate your chakra bridge point complete the following sum:(a) total of all parts divided by (b) possible maximum score of = _____ Solar Plexus Chakra Bridge Point

Take some time to reflect. You may like to note in your journal what the current ratings are and have a think about how this is manifesting in your life. Awareness and a will to change are major ingredients required to make positive and lasting change. You may notice if you have any areas with a score above eight, that these are areas in your life that you are getting the results you desire or if not you will be well on the way to having the desired outcome. Areas that scored under eight are the areas that you can focus on to create the energy flow and space required to create momentum to move in the desired direction towards your ideal flow.

If all parts selected exceed a score of 8 out of 10, this would indicate that you are achieving your ideal flow for this particular chakra and may wish to revisit this chakra in the Reinventing

Your Ideal Flow chapter, once you have reached your ideal flow in all other areas.

What we will be working towards are rankings of eight to ten for all of the parts that form the whole.

You have created movement and have started the energy moving in the direction of your choice in the Solar Plexus Chakra. You are creating and are within reach of determining the outcome.

Heart Chakra

Refer to the statement and words in the table below to come up with your chakra state; your bridge point.

Select one statement, one word or one phrase for each part of the Heart Chakra that best represents the current status of your Heart Chakra. Be honest with yourself and don't overthink what comes up.

The parts that make up the Heart Chakra correspond to the number of petals, which is twelve, or it can be half of that which is six; this is recommended if you are starting out on your journey. It may also be as many parts as you feel are required for your ideal flow in the Heart Chakra once you become familiar with the Chakra Mindset concept.

Positive	Part Selected	Shadow Aspect	Part Selected
Loving	☐	Neglectful	☐
Loved	☐	Hated	☐
Inner peace	☐	Inner turmoil	☐
Inner joy	☐	Disappointed	☐
Compassionate	☐	Unfeeling	☐
Understanding	☐	Uncaring	☐
Forgiving	☐	Difficult / resentful	☐
Accepting	☐	Defiant	☐
Trusting	☐	Suspicious	☐

I am enough	☐	I am not enough	☐
I am healed	☐	I am sick	☐
I am free	☐	I am trapped	☐
I am worthy	☐	Unworthy	☐
I am beautiful	☐	I am ugly	☐
I am whole	☐	I am broken	☐
I love myself	☐	I hate myself	☐
I am genuine	☐	I am fake	☐
I empathise	☐	I do not have empathy for others	☐
I enjoy being inti-mate	☐	I am afraid of inti-macy	☐
I am moving for-ward	☐	I am stuck	☐
I feel	☐	I do not feel	☐
I am accepting	☐	I am judgmental	☐
I deserve	☐	I do not deserve	☐

Have a look at the words and phrases you have selected. If they sit on the positive side of the chart, write them into the petal parts on the diagram provided.

If they fall under the shadow side of the chart look at the corresponding positive side and decide if the phrase or word resonates with you, or is a good indication of how you would like to feel or how you would like your reality to be. If so, replace the shadow phrase or word with the corresponding positive aspect. If not, have a look at the remainder of the words and phrases on the positive side of the chart and select one that resonates with what you would like your reality to be. Once you have selected a positive word or phrase to replace the shadow word or phrase write it in the petal parts provided.

Go through each of your selected parts and rank them from 1 to 10 to gain an understanding of how this part is currently manifesting your reality i.e. if you chose Free as a part and you find yourself at times feeling trapped you may choose to rank it as a 4. 1 = Long way to go / 10 = I am there.

Use your results from the previous point to complete the calculations below in order to find your bridge point.

(a) Heart Chakra Bridge Point (total of your selected parts that you have scored out of 10):_____

(b) Possible maximum score of : _____

If you used six petals the maximum score is 60

If you used twelve petals the maximum score is 120

If you used a number in-between the maximum score is the total of the petals times 10 (petals x 10)

In order to calculate your current bridge point complete the following sum:(a) total of all parts divided by (b) possible maximum score of = _____ Heart Chakra Bridge Point

Take some time to reflect. You may like to note in your journal what the current ratings are and have a think about how this is manifesting in your life. Awareness and a will to change are major ingredients required to make positive and lasting change. You may notice if you have any areas with a score above eight, that these are areas in your life that you are getting the results you desire or if not you will be well on the way to having the desired outcome. Areas that scored under eight are the areas that you can focus on to create the energy flow and space required to create momentum to move in the desired direction towards your ideal flow.

If all parts selected exceed a score of 8 out of 10, this would indicate that you are achieving your ideal flow for this particular chakra and may wish to revisit this chakra in the Reinventing Your Ideal Flow chapter, once you have reached your ideal flow in all other areas.

What we will be working towards are rankings of eight to ten for all of the parts that form the whole.

You have created movement and have started the energy moving in the direction of your choice in the Heart Chakra. You are creating and are within reach of determining the outcome.

Throat Chakra

Refer to the statement and words in the table below to come up with your chakra state; your bridge point.

Select one statement, one word or one phrase for each part of the Throat Chakra that best represents the current status of your Throat Chakra. Be honest with yourself and don't overthink what comes up.

The parts that make up the Throat Chakra correspond to the number of petals, which is sixteen or it can be half of that which is eight; this is recommended if you are starting out on your journey. It may also be as many parts as you feel are required for your ideal flow in the Throat Chakra once you become familiar with the Chakra Mindset concept.

Positive	Part Selected	Shadow Aspect	Part Selected
Expressive	☐	Repressed	☐
Good communicator	☐	Poor communicator	☐
Speak the truth	☐	Lie	☐
Speak the truth	☐	Afraid to speak the truth	☐
Good listener	☐	Poor listener	☐
Powerful	☐	Manipulated	☐
Safe	☐	Scared	☐

Centred	☐	Scattered	☐
Joyful	☐	Sorrowful	☐
Happy	☐	Sad	☐
Trust intuition	☐	Question my intuition	☐
Rational	☐	Irrational	☐
Honest	☐	Dishonest	☐
Listened to / heard	☐	Not heard	☐
Contribute	☐	Do not contribute	☐
Sharing	☐	Internal	☐
Valued	☐	Not valued	☐
I empathise	☐	I do not have empathy for others	☐
Talkative	☐	I am afraid of speaking	☐
Mindful of what I say	☐	Gossip	☐

Have a look at the words and phrases you have selected. If they sit on the positive side of the chart, write them into the petal parts on the diagram provided.

If they fall under the shadow side of the chart look at the corresponding positive side and decide if the phrase or word resonates with you, or is a good indication of how you would like to feel or how you would like your reality to be. If so, replace the shadow phrase or word with the corresponding positive aspect. If not, have a look at the remainder of the words and phrases on the positive side of the chart and select one that resonates with what you would like your reality to be. Once you have selected a positive word or phrase to replace the shadow word or phrase write it in the petal parts provided.

Go through each of your selected parts and rank them from 1 to 10 to gain an understanding of how this part is currently manifesting your reality i.e. if you chose Expressive as a part and you are very comfortable expressing yourself you may choose to rank it as a 9.

1 = Long way to go / 10 = I am there.

Use your results from the point above to complete the calculations below in order to find your bridge point.

(a) Throat Chakra Bridge Point (total of your selected parts that you have scored out of 10): _____

(b) Possible maximum score of: _____
If you used eight petals the maximum score is 80
If you used sixteen petals the maximum score is 160
If you used a number in-between the maximum score is the total of the petals times 10 (petals x 10)

In order to calculate your current bridge point complete the following sum:(a) total of all parts divided by (b) possible maximum score of = _____ Throat Chakra Bridge Point

Take some time to reflect, you may like to note in your journal what the current ratings are and have a think about how this is manifesting in your life. Awareness and a will to change are major ingredients required to make positive and lasting change. You may notice if you have any areas with a score above eight, that these are areas in your life that you are getting the results you desire or if not you will be well on the way to having the desired outcome. Areas that scored under eight are the areas that you can focus on to create the energy flow and space required to create momentum to move in the desired direction towards your ideal flow.

If all parts selected exceed a score of 8 out of 10, this would indicate that you are achieving your ideal flow for this particular chakra and may wish to revisit this chakra in the Reinventing Your Ideal Flow chapter, once you have reached your ideal flow in all other areas.

What we will be working towards are rankings of eight to ten for all of the parts that form the whole.

You have created movement and have started the energy moving in the direction of your choice in the Throat Chakra. You are creating and are within reach of determining the outcome.

Third Eye Chakra

Refer to the statement and words in the table below to come up with your chakra state; your bridge point.

Select one statement, one word or one phrase for each part of the Third Eye Chakra that best represents the current status of your Third Eye Chakra. Be honest with yourself and don't over-think what comes up.

The parts that make up the Third Eye Chakra correspond to the number of petals, which is two, or can be half of that which is one; this is recommended if you are starting out on your journey. It may also be as many parts as you feel are required for your ideal flow in the Third Eye Chakra once you become familiar with the Chakra Mindset concept.

Positive	Part Selected	Shadow Aspect	Part Selected
Intuitive	☐	Blocked	☐
Wise	☐	Foolish	☐
Imaginative	☐	Uncreative	☐
Insightful	☐	Unperceptive	☐
Confident	☐	Lack confidence	☐
Trusting	☐	Suspicious	☐
Light	☐	Dark	☐
Truthful	☐	Dishonest	☐
Trust inner voice	☐	Doubt inner guidance	☐
Connected	☐	Alone	☐

Purposeful	☐	Scattered	☐
Embrace potential	☐	Sabotage potential	☐
Seek out opportunity	☐	Look for excuses	☐
Clear thinker	☐	Foggy headed	☐
Clairvoyant	☐	Delusional	☐
Focused	☐	Lack of focus	☐

Have a look at the words and phrases you have selected. If they sit on the positive side of the chart, write them into the petal parts on the diagram provided.

If they fall under the shadow side of the chart look at the corresponding positive side and decide if the phrase or word resonates with you, or is a good indication of how you would like to feel or how you would like your reality to be. If so, replace the shadow phrase or word with the corresponding positive aspect. If not, have a look at the remainder of the words and phrases on the positive side of the chart and select one that resonates with what you would like your reality to be. Once you have selected a positive word or phrase to replace the shadow word or phrase write it in the petal parts provided.

Go through each of your selected parts and rank them from 1 to 10 to gain an understanding of how this part is currently manifesting your reality i.e. if you chose Confident as a part and you find yourself being self-conscious in certain circumstances you may choose to rank it as a 5.

1 = Long way to go / 10 = I am there.

Use your results from the point above to complete the calculations below in order to find your bridge point.

(a) Third Eye Chakra Bridge Point (total of your selected parts that you have scored out of 10):_____

(b) Possible maximum score of : _____

If you used one petal the maximum score is 10

If you used two petals the maximum score is 20

In order to calculate your current bridge point complete the following sum:(a) total of all parts divided by (b) possible maximum score of = _____ Third Eye Chakra Bridge Point.

Take some time to reflect. You may like to note in your journal what the current ratings are and have a think about how this is manifesting in your life. Awareness and a will to change are major ingredients required to make positive and lasting change. You may notice if you have any areas with a score above eight, that these are areas in your life that you are getting the results you desire or if not you will be well on the way to having the desired outcome. Areas that scored under eight are the areas that you can focus on to create the energy flow and space required to create momentum to move in the desired direction towards your ideal flow.

If all parts selected exceed a score of 8 out of 10, this would indicate that you are achieving your ideal flow for this particular chakra and may wish to revisit this chakra in the Reinventing Your Ideal Flow chapter, once you have reached your ideal flow in all other areas.

What we will be working towards are rankings of eight to ten for all of the parts that form the whole.

You have created movement and have started the energy moving in the direction of your choice in the Third Eye Chakra, you are creating and are within reach of determining the outcome.

Crown Chakra

Refer to the statement and words in the table below to come up with your chakra state; your bridge point.

Select one statement, one word or one phrase for each part of the Crown Chakra that best represents the current status of your Crown Chakra. Be honest with yourself and don't overthink what comes up.

The parts that make up the Crown Chakra correspond to the number of petals, which is two, or can be half of that which is one; this is recommended if you are starting out on your journey. It may also be as many parts as you feel are required for your ideal flow in the Crown Chakra once you become familiar with the Chakra Mindset concept.

Positive	Part Selected	Shadow Aspect	Part Selected
Spiritual	☐	Overly focused on the physical	☐
Consciousness	☐	Unconsciousness	☐
Pure bliss	☐	Cold	☐
Knowing	☐	Denial	☐

Wise	☐	Arrogant	☐
Liberated	☐	Imprisoned	☐
Connected	☐	Alone	☐
One with the universe /creator	☐	Alone	☐
Vibrant	☐	Dull	☐
Joyful	☐	Sad	☐
Purpose	☐	Drifting	☐
Devoted	☐	Unenthusiastic	☐
Faithful	☐	Untrustworthy	☐
Grateful	☐	Selfish	☐
Inspired	☐	Unmotivated	☐
Truth	☐	Lie	☐

Have a look at the words and phrases you have selected. If they sit on the positive side of the chart, write them into the petal parts on the diagram provided.

If they fall under the shadow side of the chart look at the corresponding positive side and decide if the phrase or word resonates with you, or is a good indication of how you would like to feel or how you would like your reality to be. If so, replace the shadow phrase or word with the corresponding positive aspect. If not, have a look at the remainder of the words and phrases on the positive side of the chart and select one that resonates with what you would like your reality to be. Once you have selected a positive word or phrase to replace the shadow word or phrase write it in the petal parts provided.

Go through each of your selected parts and rank them from 1 to 10 to gain an understanding of how this part is currently manifesting your reality i.e. if you chose Liberated as a part and you find yourself feeling quite liberated you could may rank it as a 8.

1 = Long way to go / 10 = I am there.

Use your results from the point above to complete the calculations below in order to find your bridge point.

    (a) Crown Chakra Bridge Point (total of your selected parts that you have scored out of 10):_____

    (b) Possible maximum score of:_____

If you used one petal the maximum score is 10

If you used two petals the maximum score is 20

In order to calculate your current bridge point complete the following sum:(a) total of all parts divided by (b) possible maximum score of = _____ Crown Chakra Bridge Point.

Take some time to reflect, you may like to note in your journal what the current ratings are and have a think about how this is manifesting in your life. Awareness and a will to change are major ingredients required to make positive and lasting change. You may notice if you have any areas with a score above eight, that these are areas in your life that you are getting the results you desire or if not you will be well on the way to having the desired outcome. Areas that scored under eight are the areas that you can focus on to create the energy flow and space required to create momentum to move in the desired direction towards your ideal flow.

If all parts selected exceed a score of 8 out of 10, this would indicate that you are achieving your ideal flow for this particular chakra and may wish to revisit this chakra in the Reinventing Your Ideal Flow chapter, once you have reached your ideal flow in all other areas.

What we will be working towards are rankings of eight to ten for all of the parts that form the whole.

You have created movement and have started the energy moving in the direction of your choice in the Crown Chakra, you are creating and are within reach of determining the outcome.

Bridge Point Table

In the table below record your bridge point for all chakras. It is recommended that initially you work systematically from the Root Chakra up to the Crown Chakra.

It is recommended that you read through each of the chakra chapters and consider your current bridge point before getting started.

Chakra	Bridge Point	Sequence
Root (Belonging & Survival)	Current Bridge Point _____%	1
Sacral (Sensuality & Pleasure)	Current Bridge Point _____%	2
Solar Plexus (Personal Power)	Current Bridge Point _____%	3
Heart (Relationships)	Current Bridge Point _____%	4
Throat (Communication)	Current Bridge Point _____%	5
Third Eye (Intuition)	Current Bridge Point _____%	6
Crown (Spirituality)	Current Bridge Point _____%	7

Journal

Chapter 11

Getting into Your Ideal Flow

Now that you have completed working through the activating your Chakra Mindset stage and have completed your chakra state analysis exercise, it is time to get started on creating your ideal flow.

The individual chakra chapters provide information on the chakras as well as exercises, techniques and rituals for you to become familiar with, explore and create an individualised action plan for yourself as you are working with a particular chakra during the getting into your ideal flow period.

The amount of time spent working through this stage of the program will be approximately seven weeks.

NB: If you scored above 80% in some areas we recommend that you still work through each of the chakras consecutively from the Root Chakra to the Crown Chakra in order to become familiar with the program and concepts.

Recognising and Challenging Limiting Beliefs

What is a limiting belief? A limiting belief is something that we tell ourselves and we accept as truth. Limiting beliefs are formed based on many factors including: upbringing, environment, education and past experiences. Some common limiting beliefs for each chakra can be found in the individual chakra chapters.

Have a look through the list of examples of limiting beliefs for the relevant chakra and write down any that you relate to or that ring true for you. Alternatively you may have a limiting belief that has held you back that is not listed. Please write any limiting beliefs in your *Journal*

In order to gain further insight to your current beliefs that may be holding you back, we have created the limiting beliefs release technique that can be found on the guided energy intention techniques CD or mp3 download. The limiting beliefs exercise will take you on a guided expedition to identify any limiting beliefs, collect them and prepare to let them go.

Once you have completed this exercise, revisit your limiting beliefs that you had previously listed and see if you have identified any additional beliefs. Now ask yourself the following questions in regards to each limiting belief:

❦ How do I know this?

❦ Who says so?

Processing these questions will start to loosen the structures that have held these beliefs firm.

Once you have answered these questions, move on to the following set of questions:

- What will things look like when I no longer have these beliefs?
- What will it feel like?
- What will it sound, smell and taste like?

Creating the Goal

Goals are a great way of setting your intentions and creating a visual; a road map to your desired outcome. In order for goal setting to be effective you need to be able to imagine yourself having what you want in order to achieve it. I work with many people who know what they want, but until they can imagine themselves, see themselves and feel themselves with the desired outcome, they have not been able to manifest positive change. Once you can truly imagine the outcome it then becomes something that is within your reach. Alas, there is more to goal setting than this; being able to imagine the outcome is the first step, now it's time to work on the how. What steps do you need to take in order to get the energy flowing towards your ideal outcome?

I have worked with many a client who has said, "I can see it so clearly, I sit and I visualise, I paint the perfect picture of what I want, but nothing happens." When I ask what action they have taken to move towards the outcome that is when they realise there is more to manifestation than just design. Although imagination and design is the first, and the most crucial component to goal setting, creating and implementing action plans is also a vital component of the process. You also need to have behavioural flexibility to change your behaviour if it is not moving you in the desired direction.

You will be setting a mini goal for up to three petals or parts of the chakra you are working on. The goals are intended to be mini goals as steps to work towards your ideal flow for each chakra (i.e. if you are working on the Root Chakra and one of your parts is about physical health, perhaps your mini goal for this petal would be to walk for 15 minutes per day for the duration of your getting into your ideal flow stage whilst working with the Root Chakra).

Create a picture of the desired part and bring it to life. Ask yourself the following questions:

- What will things look like when I achieve my mini goal?
- What will it feel like?
- What will it sound, smell and taste like?
- How will I know when I'm there?

 Journal

With any goal setting process remember that the goals you set need to be SMART:

❧ Specific – Be clear about what you want to achieve! Who, what, when, where, why

❧ Measurable – How will you know that your goal has been achieved? Ensure that progress can be measured

❧ Attainable – Is your goal realistic? Is it something you want to work towards? Is the time frame appropriate? Any goal can be achieved if it is made attainable

❧ Realistic – A realistic goal has a specific, measurable, attainable, and timed outcome, which you are both willing and able to work towards

❧ Timed – Every goal must have a time frame; an end date. Without a time frame you are giving your unconscious mind permission to be lazy. With a time frame in place your unconscious mind immediately goes into action, knowing that the end date is getting nearer

NB: Examples of SMART goals can be found within the individual chakra chapters.

Once you have completed this process for the parts within the chakra that you are working on, I would like you to imagine the whole; the result of all of the pieces coming together to form your ideal flow within the chakra once you have reached all of your mini goals.

See the centre of the chakra when all of the pieces have come together to create your ideal flow.

Visualisation Exercises

Exercise One

You can complete the following visualisation exercise by reading through the exercise below or refer to the energy intentions techniques CD or mp3 download and complete the exercises as directed on the audio.

This goal setting and visualisation exercise was adapted from the NLP goal setting and anchoring techniques created by Richard Bandler and John Grinder.

Setting the Scene

Stand in a quiet, private spot and bring the picture of your ideal flow to life in your mind. Imagine you are holding a picture of your desired outcome when all the pieces and all your petals have come together and you are looking at yourself in the picture; make the picture bright, sharp and focused. Imagine how you would be feeling, and notice all of the things you would be experiencing through each of your senses.

Now I want you to step into the picture so you are seeing what you would be seeing through your own eyes. Feel what you would be feeling; hear what you would be hearing. What would you be telling yourself? Get fully associated into the state (seeing things through your eyes). Once you are there I would like you to step back out of the picture, hold it in your hands and breathe three huge breaths into it, bringing it to life.

Imagine yourself having achieved your ideal flow. I want you to release the image and watch it float out into the future to the specific time and place where you will be when you reach it. As you do that, I want you to feel those feelings of accomplishment, see again what is around you and notice where you are and any sounds that you may be hearing. I want you to place your hands on the location of the specific chakra you are working on and firmly holding those feelings, thoughts, pictures and sounds in the chakra area. Place the energy and intention into the chakra, allow yourself to feel the flow and allow it to start working towards your desired outcome.

Taking three deep breaths, allow yourself to come back to the present.

Notice how attractive, attainable and real the outcome has now become.

Now ask yourself this last set of questions:

❦ What do I need to learn in order to reach my goal?
❦ What do I need to do in order to reach my goal?

❧ What currently prevents me from reaching my goal?

❧ What will I do to overcome what prevents me from reaching my goal?

You now have all the answers and information you will need to start moving forward in the direction of your choice.

You may be telling yourself that if you knew the answers to these questions you would already be having the results you desire. By doing this you are giving yourself permission to fail, or perhaps not even try.

Exercise Two

Imagine talking to yourself once you have created your ideal flow. What things could you learn? In order to gain further insight into what steps will work for you, we have created the advice from someone who knows exercise. This exercise has been adapted from the anxiety timeline technique in Neuro-Linguistic Programing originally created by Tad James and more recently updated by Pip MacKay. The exercise will take you on a guided journey.

Hindsight is a wonderful thing, imagine having it prior to doing something.

You can complete the following visualisation exercise by reading through the exercise below or refer to the energy intention techniques CD or mp3 download and complete the advice from someone who knows exercise as directed on the audio.

Advice from Someone Who Knows

Imagine yourself floating out to the future, to the time in space where you are exactly as you have imagined and designed yourself to be. Your state is as you'd imagined, your ideal flow has been achieved, your bridge point is a distant memory; you have come a long way since you started this journey.

You are whole and you are living in the moment, as it should be.

Imagine yourself observing this future you and spend some time watching, observing, and enjoying the outcome. Feel the feelings of accomplishment, success and achievement.

It's OK to celebrate what you have done, you deserve it.

Watch yourself interacting, thinking, breathing and living; doing exactly what you had planned. Could it be that it even exceeds what you had imagined possible?

Now I'd like you to stand beside your future self and have a conversation. Give your future self a hug and acknowledge your dedication, commitment and how far you have come.

Now I'd like you to ask your future self some questions:

- How did you get here?
- What did you do differently?
- What did you do consistently?
- What else do I need to know?

As you listen to the answers, you ensure that the advice is going deep, deep into your unconscious mind, so that when you start to do these things they will seem familiar, they will seem right and they will come easily.

Now I would like you to notice what you're feeling.

Can you feel the energy? Radiating through your future self, your aura is expanding and mingling with your current self.

Do you feel the flow, the excitement and that sense of purpose?

You feel all these wonderful things, and it is exactly how you had envisaged it to be.

Now I'd like you to slowly, with those feelings of excitement and giddy anticipation, come back to where you are now in the room and notice that you have brought those wonderful feelings back into the room with you; they have mingled with your present state, giving you a taste, a teaser, an insight into what lies ahead when you choose to follow through.

Journal

Once you have completed the exercise record your findings in your journal, reflecting on what you have learnt and what needs to be done. Does your goal or action plan need to be modified based on what you have observed during this exercise?

Focused Intention Technique

The aim of completing the focused intention technique is for you to be able to create a desired feeling at any time. This is achieved by recalling a specific event that reflects the desired state, and applying a stimulus at the peak of the state linking that state and the stimulus neurologically.

Journal

It is recommended that you read through the steps below before completing the focused intention technique. If you have the energy intention techniques CD or mp3 download it will guide you through the process. It is recommended that you read through the process to familiarise yourself with the technique prior to listening to the audio. The following elements are crucial to completing this technique effectively.

1. Recall or imagine a vivid experience that gives you the feeling you will have once you achieve your ideal flow in the chakra part you are working with. If you feel you have never felt the feeling you are aiming for you can imagine what it would feel like. The greater you are able to recall or imagine how you felt, what you saw, what you heard and anything you may have been telling yourself, the more intense the state will be for you to successfully do this exercise. On the audio you will be prompted to turn the feeling up; imagine a volume switch located in the chakra area you are working on and when you are recalling or

193

imagining the state I would like you to turn up the volume (the intensity) of the feeling by visualising or feeling the chakra spinning in the direction that it would need to go to increase the intensity.

2. Provide a specific stimulus as per the stimulus diagram that corresponds with the chakra you are working on, see the focused intention technique diagram and step by step instructions in each of the chakra sections for the correct chakra point location. At the peak of that feeling (see chart below) apply the stimulus and hold for a count of five to ten whilst it is at its peak, and release.

Applying the Stimulus - Timing

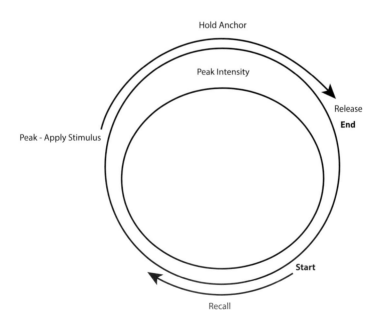

Please refer to the individual chakra section for an image and examples of states to use for each of the chakras.

The following is the process you will follow to complete the focused intention technique.

1. Close your eyes take three deep breaths and relax, remember a time when you felt totally _____ (insert state).

2. Allow your mind to drift back to that event, and as you go back to that time now, see what you saw, hear what you heard, and really feel the feelings of being totally _____.

3. Place your hand on your chakra point (as per the diagram in the chakra chapter you are working on) applying pressure with two fingers. As you apply pressure imagine the chakra spinning in the direction that it needs to go in order to intensify the feeling; like turning up a volume switch.

4. Allow yourself to feel the energy, recall the feelings and really experience the sensations whilst you are at the peak of the state. When the feelings start to subside, remove your fingers from the chakra point.

5. Open your eyes and take three deep breaths and start on the next state for the chakra you are working on repeating steps 1 to 4.

6. Once you have stacked the required number of states, relax your shoulders and apply pressure to test your chakra point. Allow yourself to feel and enjoy the sensations.

Use your chakra point to kick off your daily physical rituals or any time you feel that you need a boost.

Once you have completed the three energy intention techniques it is time to design the getting into your ideal flow action plan for the time you will be working with a specific chakra.

All exercises and rituals are explained in detail in the individual chakra chapters.

The table below can be found in your Chakra Mindset Journal. If you do not have access to the journal it can be downloaded via the web or you can create your own Getting into Your Ideal Flow Action Plan as per the template below.

 Journal

Getting into Your Ideal Flow Action Plan

	Individual Plan
Smart Goals – Mini Goals, Actions (recommended during your getting into your ideal flow stage) Write down one to two actions you will take during the getting into your ideal flow stage for each of your mini goals.	Mini Goal: Actions 1. 2. Mini Goal: Actions 1. 2. Mini Goal Actions 1. 2.

Gratitude Practice (recommended as part of your morning moments practice) Design what you would like to include in your gratitude practice (use examples provided under each of the individual chakra chapters; you can add additional things if you choose to).	I am grateful for: 1. 2. 3.
Mantra Practice (recommended as part of your morning moments process) Create at least three mantras that you will work with for the chakra you are focusing on as detailed in the individual chakra chapter. You can have as many as you like; we recommend a minimum of three. The mantras should be included into your morning moments. You can also choose to incorporate your mantra practice at other times of the day such as before or after your guided meditation process or at any other time during the day that you feel you require a boost.	1 2. 3.

Essential Oils (individual discretion) Have a look through the essential oils recommended for each chakra and select one or two to work with for the getting into your ideal flow stage.	1. 2.
Crystals (individual discretion) Have a look through the recommended crystals listed under each of the individual chakra chapters and choose one of the crystals to work with for the getting into your ideal flow stage.	1.

Focused Intention Technique (recommended as part of your daily physical rituals) To start off your daily physical rituals spend some time reflecting on your desired outcomes and trigger your chakra point by applying pressure to the chakra you are working with. List the three states you selected for the chakra you are working with when you created your chakra point. You do not have to repeat the set up process, you simply apply pressure to your chakra point and allow the sensations to flow through your body for a minute or so, whilst allowing your focus to settle on the chakra point.	When setting up my chakra point I recalled and used a time that I felt really: 1. 2. 3.

Physical Exercises (recommended during the getting into your ideal flow stage) Choose one of the physical activities to include in your getting into your ideal flow stage	1.
Yoga Poses (recommended as part of your daily physical rituals) Explore the yoga poses recommended for the chakra you will be working with and list them to include in your daily physical rituals for the getting into your ideal flow stage.	1. 2.
Other Activities (recommended during the getting into your ideal flow stage) Choose two activities from the other activities section of the individual chakra chapter to incorporate into your getting into your ideal flow plan.	1. 2.

Guided Meditation (recommended each day during the getting into your ideal flow stage) Listen to the guided meditation for the chakra you are working on. This can be done at any time of the day. However, I would recommend doing it in the evening before bed or in the morning if you have enough time. List your preferred time of day that you would like to schedule in your meditation.	1.

The following is an example of a completed Getting into Your Ideal Flow Action Plan using the Root Chakra as the chakra to be worked with.

	Individual Plan – Example Root Chakra
Smart Goals – Mini Goals Actions (recommended during your getting into your ideal flow stage) Write down one to two actions you will take during the getting into your ideal flow stage for each of your mini goals.	Mini Goal: Part – Good Relationship with Money Goal – To create a monthly budget for use to manage household funds. The budget will take into consideration all expenses and income and give me the opportunity to accurately record transactions. I will complete this budget by Friday of this week. Actions 1. Create budget template 2. List all regular income and expenses
Gratitude Practice (recommended as part of your morning moments practice) Design what you would like to include in your gratitude practice (use examples provided under each of the individual chakra chapters; you can add additional things if you choose to).	I am grateful for: 1. My Health 2. My Home 3. My Job

Mantra Practice (recommended as part of your morning moments process) Create at least three mantras that you will work with for the chakra you are focusing on as detailed in the individual chakra chapter. You can have as many as you like; we recommend a minimum of three. The mantras should be included into your morning moments. You can also choose to incorporate your mantra practice at other times of the day such as before or after your guided meditation process or at any other time during the day that you feel you require a boost.	1. Belonging – I Belong 2. Abundant – I am Abundant 3. Grounded – I am Grounded
Essential Oils (individual discretion) Have a look through the essential oils recommended for each chakra and select one or two to work with for the getting into your ideal flow stage.	1.Sandalwood 2.Clove

Crystals (individual discretion) Have a look through the recommended crystals listed under each of the individual chakra chapters and choose one of the crystals to work with for the getting into your ideal flow stage.	1.Ruby
Focused Intention Technique (recommended as part of your daily physical rituals) To start off your daily physical rituals spend some time reflecting on your desired outcomes, and trigger your chakra point by applying pressure to the chakra you are working with. List the three states you selected for the chakra you are working with, when you created your chakra point. You do not have to repeat the set up process; you simply apply pressure to your chakra point and allow the sensations to flow through your body for a minute or so, whilst allowing your focus to settle on the chakra point.	When setting up my chakra point I recalled and used a time that I felt really: 1.Healthy 2.Worthy 3.Connected to nature

Physical Exercises (recommended during the getting into your ideal flow stage)	1. Go for a walk in nature
Other Activities (recommended during the getting into your ideal flow stage) Choose two activities from the other activities section of the individual chakra chapter to incorporate into your getting into your ideal flow plan.	1. Gardening 2. Mindful eating
Guided Meditation (recommended each day during the getting into your ideal flow stage) Listen to the guided meditation for the chakra you are working on. This can be done at any time of the day. However, I would recommend doing it in the evening before bed or in the morning if you have enough time. List your preferred time of day that you would like to schedule in your meditation.	1. I will do my Root Chakra guided meditation before I go to sleep for each night I am working with my Root Chakra.

Chapter 12

Maintaining Your Ideal Flow

Now that you have created your ideal flow we can start thinking about maintenance and how you can maintain the flow that you have created. Your results will be easier to maintain once you have decided on a maintenance plan.

When you started working through the program we referred to your starting point as your bridge point. Now you have spent time working with and becoming familiar with each of your chakras we are evaluating your chakra state based on your land point. This is where you are now that you have started your journey, made your way across the bridge, and have reached your land point.

All successful people have a routine or rituals that enable them to stay on top of the game, that help them to maintain their lifestyles and the success that they have created. As mentioned earlier in the book, there is not and nor should there be, a point of completion if you want to feel stimulated and excited about your life. Many people make the mistake of switching off once they have reached a goal or a milestone, inadvertently slipping back into old patterns. It is imperative that at this point you evaluate where you are and decide on the actions and the routines that you will implement in order to maintain what you have created.

Having spent the past weeks working though the program and becoming familiar with your chakras, you will have found that there are certain areas of your life that you feel are more important to you than other areas; these are areas that you will need to continue to pay attention to. There will also be areas of your life which are not so important to you but still require your attention to ensure that the energy in these areas does not become stagnant, therefore interrupting your ideal flow.

Now is the time to reflect back on your bridge point, celebrate what you have achieved and prioritise each area of your life. Remember it may be unrealistic to expect that you will be performing in all areas of your life at 100%, but by now you will have a healthy understanding of the need to pay attention to all areas of your life in order to maintain your ideal flow.

What you should be looking for in the current land point state analysis is an increase on your bridge point percentage. If you find that it is the same as or lower than your bridge point it is recommended that you spend an additional seven days working through the getting into your ideal flow stage for that particular chakra.

You will need to redo the Chakra State Analysis based on the parts that you had originally selected for each of your chakras to see where you sit after having spent time working with and becoming more familiar with your chakras.

Journal

Repeat the following process for each of your chakras. There is space in your journal to calculate your land point; alternatively you can do the analysis online at www.chakramindset.com, or you can use the space in this book prior to deciding on your maintenance plan.

Chakra State Analysis – Land Point

Please consider your state of mind or mood when doing the Chakra State Analysis to determine your land point. Aim to complete the Chakra State Analysis when you have at least half an hour of quiet time, so that you do not feel rushed.

Make sure you use your journal for reflection and review, so that you can identify if there are any obstacles or acts of self-sabotage that you may be unconsciously acting on in order to hold yourself back. Sometimes we hold onto unpleasant states because it may serve a purpose such as giving us significance or drama in our lives. Remember you are the champion of your life, not the victim of circumstances.

Root Chakra

Go through each of your original parts and rank them from 1 to 10 to gain an understanding of how this part is currently manifesting your reality.

1 = Long way to go / 10 = I am there.

Use your results from the point above to complete the calculations below in order to find your land point.

(a) Root Chakra Land Point (total of your selected parts that you have scored out of 10):_____

(b) Possible maximum score of : _____

If you used two petals the maximum score is 20

If you used four petals the maximum score is 40

If you used a number in-between the maximum score is the total of the petals times 10 (petals x 10)

In order to calculate your land point complete the following sum:(a) total of all parts divided by (b) possible maximum score of = _____ Root Chakra Land Point.

Take some time to reflect, you may like to note in your journal what the current ratings are with today's date and have a think about how this is manifesting in your life. Notice how it has changed from your bridge point. Ask yourself these simple questions:

What is different?

How do I feel about these achievements?

Sacral Chakra

Go through each of your original parts and rank them from 1 to 10 to gain an understanding of how this part is currently manifesting your reality.

1 = Long way to go / 10 = I am there.

Use your results from the point above to complete the calculations below in order to find your land point.

(a) Sacral Chakra Land Point (total of your selected parts that you have scored out of 10): _____

(b) Possible maximum score of : _____

If you used three petals the maximum score is 30

If you used six petals the maximum score is 60

If you used a number in-between the maximum score is the total of the petals times 10 (petals x 10)

In order to calculate your current land point, complete the following sum:(a) total of all parts divided by (b) possible maximum score of = _____ Sacral Chakra Land Point.

Take some time to reflect. You may like to note in your journal what the current ratings are with today's date and have a think about how this is manifesting in your life. Notice how it has changed from your bridge point. Ask yourself these simple questions:

What is different?

How do I feel about these achievements?

Solar Plexus Chakra

Go through each of your original parts and rank them from 1 to 10 to gain an understanding of how this part is currently manifesting your reality.

1 = Long way to go / 10 = I am there.

Use your results from the point above to complete the calculations below in order to find your land point.

(a) Solar Plexus Chakra Land Point (total of your selected parts that you have scored out of 10): _____

(b) Possible maximum score of: _____

If you used five petals the maximum score is 50

If you used ten petals the maximum score is 100

If you used a number in-between the maximum score is the total of the petals times 10 (petals x 10)

In order to calculate your current land point, complete the following sum:(a) total of all parts divided by (b) possible maximum score of = _____ Solar Plexus Chakra Land Point.

Take some time to reflect. You may like to note in your journal what the current ratings are with today's date and have a think about how this is manifesting in your life. Notice how it has changed from your bridge point. Ask yourself these simple questions:

What is different?
How do I feel about these achievements?

Heart Chakra

Go through each of your original parts and rank them from 1 to 10 to gain an understanding of how this part is currently manifesting your reality.
1 = Long way to go / 10 = I am there.

Use your results from the point above to complete the calculations below in order to find your land point.

(a) Heart Chakra Land Point (total of your selected parts that you have scored out of 10): _____

(b) Possible maximum score of: _____
If you used six petals the maximum score is 60
If you used twelve petals the maximum score is 120
If you used a number in-between the maximum score is the total of the petals times 10 (petals x 10)

In order to calculate your current land point, complete the following sum: (a) total of all parts divided by (b) possible maximum score of

= _____ Heart Chakra Land Point.

Take some time to reflect. You may like to note in your journal what the current ratings are with today's date and have a think about how this is manifesting in your life. Notice how it has changed from your bridge point. Ask yourself these simple questions:

What is different?

How do I feel about these achievements?

Throat Chakra

Go through each of your selected parts and rank them from 1 to 10 to gain an understanding of how this part is currently manifesting your reality

1 = Long way to go / 10 = I am there.

Use your results from the point above to complete the calculations below in order to find your land point.

(a) Throat Chakra Land Point (total of your selected parts that you have scored out of 10): _____

(b) Possible maximum score of: _____

If you used eight petals the maximum score is 80

If you used sixteen petals the maximum score is 160

If you used a number in-between the maximum score is the total of the petals times 10 (petals x 10)

In order to calculate your current land point, complete the following sum:(a) total of all parts divided by (b) possible maximum score of = _____ Throat Chakra Land Point.

Take some time to reflect. You may like to note in your journal what the current ratings are with today's date and have a think about how this is manifesting in your life. Notice how it has changed from your bridge point. Ask yourself these simple questions:

What is different?
How do I feel about these achievements?

Third Eye Chakra

Go through each of your original parts and rank them from 1 to 10 to gain an understanding of how this part is currently manifesting your reality.

1 = Long way to go / 10 = I am there.

Use your results from the point above to complete the calculations below in order to find your land point.

(a) Third Eye Chakra Land Point (total of your selected parts that you have scored out of 10): _____
(b) Possible maximum score of:_____
    If you used one petal the maximum score is 10
    If you used two petals the maximum score is 20

In order to calculate your current land point, complete the following sum:(a) total of all parts divided by (b) possible maximum score of = _____ Third Eye Chakra Land Point.

Take some time to reflect. You may like to note in your journal what the current ratings are with today's date and have a think about how this is manifesting in your life. Notice how it has changed from your bridge point. Ask yourself these simple questions:

What is different?

How do I feel about these achievements?

Crown Chakra

Go through each of your original parts and rank them from 1 to 10 to gain an understanding of how this part is currently manifesting your reality.

1 = Long way to go / 10 = I am there.

Use your results from the point above to complete the calculations below in order to find your land point.

(a) Crown Chakra Land Point (total of your selected parts that you have scored out of 10): _____

(b) Possible maximum score of: _____

If you used one petal the maximum score is 10

If you used two petals the maximum score is 20

In order to calculate your current land point, complete the following sum:(a) total of all parts divided by (b) possible maximum score of = _____ Crown Chakra Land Point.

Take some time to reflect. You may like to note in your journal what the current ratings are with today's date and have a think about how this is manifesting in your life. Notice how it has changed from your bridge point. Ask yourself these simple questions:

What is different?
How do I feel about these achievements?

Now that you have spent some time revisiting the chakra state analysis to determine your land point record your findings in the following table.

The table below allows space to record your original bridge point your current land point and to prioritise the focus intent across the chakras to suit your ideal flow.

When completing the prioritisation exercise remember that although it is important to have flow across all chakras, you will have areas of priority based on your life journey and purpose. Rank each chakra accordingly with 1 being your highest priority through to 7.

Chakra Flow and Focus Priority

Chakra	Bridge Point	Land Point	Priority (1 to 7)
Root (Belonging & Survival)			
Sacral (Sensuality & Pleasure)			
Solar Plexus (Personal Power)			
Heart (Relationships)			
Throat (Communication)			
Third Eye (Intuition)			
Crown (Spirituality)			

Chapter 13

Creating Your Maintenance Plan

There are some points I would like you to keep in mind when creating your maintenance plan; firstly, whatever you decide to do on a regular basis needs to be sustainable. You must set yourself routines that you will be able to include in your daily activities. Your daily routines should help you maintain your land point and help move you towards achieving your goals.

The following practices, some of which you established in your creating the ideal flow process, should be maintained.

Morning Moments – Morning moments is a combination of your gratitude practice, your mantras and visualisations. The practice of morning moments gives you a great start to the day and takes minimal time to complete. The entire process takes under five minutes.

Gratitude practice – Be sure to continue with your gratitude practice, remembering the more we are grateful for, the more we will have to be grateful for.

Mantras – Continuing your daily mantras will reinforce what it is you are striving to maintain. Be sure to incorporate mantras that reflect your priorities for each of the chakras.

Visualising your ideal day – Take the time to visualise, feel and create your ideal day. Imagine feeling and seeing your interactions with others, your results and how you would like the events of the day to play out.

Meditation – I would recommend incorporating meditation in your routine, whether it be something you schedule in as a daily practice or for a few days a week. Your meditation practice need not take you half an hour or an hour to complete; incorporating five to ten minutes of meditation into your regular routine will give you the space, time and modality to connect with your inner essence.

Physical Activities

Yoga practice – Choose two to four of the yoga poses that you resonated with, again using your priority list as a guide; incorporate these into your daily activities. This can be done in the morning or evening. You may wish to expand on your yoga practice by taking a class or making the time to practice yoga independently on a regular basis (i.e. twice a week for half an hour per session).

Incorporating some of the physical activities listed in each of the individual chakra sections in your regular routine will help you to maintain your fitness and wellbeing. Again, use your priority listing and the exercises that resonated with you over the past few weeks to develop a routine.

You can revisit this as often as you like, incorporating other physical activities or increasing frequencies to correspond with your goals.

Other Activities

Colour – Incorporate the colours of each of your chakras into your wardrobe and décor; having a chakra colour day on rotation can help keep your focus and energy moving.

Crystals – Continue to use the crystals that you identified during the getting into your ideal flow period; you could meditate with them, wear them, or simply have them in your environment.

Essential oils – Continue to use the essential oils that you became familiar with during the getting into your ideal flow period; use them as required, and make them a part of your routine.

Goal actions – Be sure to incorporate actions and tasks that help you move towards any mini goals you would like to continue working on. If you have reached your mini goals, it's time to set a big goal for each of your chakras. Repeat the goal setting process for new goals.

The following is an example of a maintenance plan for someone with the following chakra area priorities:

NB: Just because something is ranked 7 does not mean it is not important. What it means is that in relation to other aspects of life this is less of a focus at this particular point in time.

Chakra Maintenance Plan (example only)

Chakra	Bridge	Land Point	Priority (1 to 7)
Root (Belonging & Survival)	75%	82%	4
Sacral (Sensuality & Pleasure)	38%	60%	6
Solar Plexus (Personal Power)	90%	90%	1
Heart (Relationships)	70%	75%	7
Throat (Communication)	60%	70%	3
Third Eye (Intuition)	82%	90%	2
Crown (Spirituality)	70%	87%	5

Action Plan

Morning Moments	All Chakras	Daily on waking
Yoga practice	Solar Plexus, Throat, Heart, Root	Daily – Cat Pose, Warrior Pose, Mountain Pose
Meditation practice	Third Eye, Crown	Daily – Evening before bed, 10 minutes
Sing in shower	Throat	At least twice a week
Massage	Heart, Sacral	At least once every three – six months
Treadmill	Heart, Root	Daily – 15 minutes
Try new things	Solar Plexus	Once a month – Even if it's just a new food or drink
Use to do list	Solar Plexus	Daily
Pilates	Solar Plexus, Root	Twice a week
Charity / community work	Heart, Crown	Once a month
Dance	Sacral, Throat	Once a month
Goal activity	All Chakras	Daily, weekly, monthly

Although the maintenance plan may appear dauntingly busy, it is actually less than an hour each day spent on balancing, reflecting and nurturing yourself. The hour can be split between morning and evening tasks if that is more sustainable for you.

Chapter 14

Reinventing Your Ideal Flow

Once you have worked with this program for some time you may begin to feel adventurous and want to aspire to achieve even greater and bigger things than you had initially identified; that's precisely the aim of this program! The techniques will assist you to gain and identify additional resources and processes that will accompany you on your journey of self-discovery and growth.

In this section of the program you will take the time to go back and evaluate your reinvented bridge point and add to the existing parts that you have selected. You may feel the need to change some of the previously selected parts, and that is also fine; remember it is OK to change your desires and priorities as your life evolves.

You will need to redo the Chakra State Analysis quiz. This time you will be using the actual number of petals for each of the chakras or even adding additional parts if you feel compelled to do so.

Be sure to use your journal to reflect on the changes and any points that you feel are relevant in regards to your revised selections.

Once you have completed the Chakra State Analysis to determine your reinvented bridge point you will need to redo the following exercises found in Chapter 11:

- Limiting beliefs release
- Creating the goal
- Advice from someone who knows
- Focused intention technique

Once this has been done for all chakras you will undertake a new getting into your ideal flow period followed by the maintaining your ideal flow process.

The Chakra Mindset is a companion for your growth; it should be used to reflect, plan and celebrate your progress and achievements as you make your way through life. Remember, there is no end point; the process evolves and grows along with you. Enjoy the ride and the rewards will be even more meaningful; for if you enjoy the process of creating and achieving, you will be more likely to continue to step things up, keeping you motivated and fulfilled. This is your life, you should have a big say in each of the chapters that comprise the story of your journey.

Recommended Resources

Chakra Workout: Balancing the chakras with yoga by Mary Horsley. Octopus Publishing Group Ltd, 2006.

Chakras: Energy Centers of Transformation by Harish Johari. Destiny Books, 2000.

Pocket Guide to Chakras by Joy Gardner-Gordon. The Crossing Press, 1998.

The Chakras by Hilary H. Carter. O-Books, 2012.

The Crystal Bible: A Definitive Guide to Crystals by Judy Hall. Godsfield Press, 2003.

Vibrational Healing through the Chakras: with Light, Color, Sound, Crystals, and Aromatherapy by Joy Gardner. Crossing Press, 2006.